Atlantic Rising

Changing Commercial Dynamics
in the Atlantic Basin

Daniel S. Hamilton
Editor

Center for Transatlantic Relations
Paul H. Nitze School of Advanced International Studies
Johns Hopkins University

Hamilton, Daniel S., ed. *Atlantic Rising: Changing Commercial Dynamics in the Atlantic Basin*

Washington, DC: Center for Transatlantic Relations, 2015.

Center for Transatlantic Relations
The Paul H. Nitze School of Advanced International Studies
The Johns Hopkins University
1717 Massachusetts Ave., NW, Suite 525
Washington, DC 20036
Tel: (202) 663-5880
Fax: (202) 663-5879
Email: transatlantic@jhu.edu
http://transatlantic.sais-jhu.edu

ISBN 978-0-9907720-3-3

Cover images: shutterstock.com/hywords; shutterstock.com/autsawin uttisin.

Contents

Preface and Acknowledgments

More commerce flows within the Atlantic Basin than any other. Never have so many workers and consumers entered the Atlantic economy as quickly or as suddenly as in the past fifteen years. Despite the rise of other powers and recent economic turbulence, North America and Europe remain the fulcrum of the world economy, each other's most important and profitable market and largest source of onshored jobs. No other commercial artery is as integrated. And while rapidly developing countries in Latin America and Africa are best known for the inexpensive goods and commodities they supply to the rest of the world, their consumers are also connecting with the global marketplace, and in coming years they will become major engines of the global economy. Parts of Africa are already among the fastest growing regions of the world. North-South American commercial ties are burgeoning, and Europe's commercial ties to both Latin America and Africa are substantial. The weakest links are those between Latin America and Africa, but those connections are also the most dynamic.

Growing commercial connections across the Atlantic Hemisphere offer considerable potential. But they are challenged by a range of developments, from stalled multilateral and bi-regional trade negotiations, domestic protectionist challenges, inequality, trade-distorting measures and absence of pan-Atlantic economic governance mechanisms. The Atlantic Hemisphere accounts for over half of global GDP, yet it is a region of extreme wealth and poverty.

Atlantic peoples are engaging and interacting in a whole host of ways that are shifting the contours of hemispheric interdependence and global power, yet relatively little attention has been paid to pan-Atlantic dynamics. With this in mind, the Center for Transatlantic Relations asked experts and seasoned practitioners to explore the changing commercial dynamics of the Atlantic Basin—the evolving economic linkages among North and South America, Africa and Europe. Our conclusions have been informed by a series of meetings we have held throughout the Atlantic Basin with eminent persons, government officials, business executives, legislators, and a range of stakeholders. We have profited from the insights gathered from those discussions and thank our interlocutors for their participation. The views expressed in this volume, however, are those of the authors alone.

This study is part of a broad-based effort by the Atlantic Basin Initiative, a public-private partnership of eminent persons, research institutions and stakeholders support sustainable growth, human development and security in the Atlantic Hemisphere.

I would like to thank Katrien Maes and Miriam Cunningham for their tremendous assistance, as well as the European Union and Telefonica for their support. None of the views expressed here, however, represent those of any government or institution.

DANIEL S. HAMILTON
Executive Director
Center for Transatlantic Relations
School of Advanced International Studies
Johns Hopkins University

Chapter 1

Merchandise Trade in the Atlantic Basin

Lorena Ruano

This chapter provides an analysis of descriptive data of merchandise trade within the Atlantic Basin between 2004 and 2012, based primarily on the information made available by the World Trade Organization (WTO).[1] Other chapters in this volume analyze services trade and investment flows, which represent other important aspects of economic exchange in the Atlantic Basin, but need to be kept conceptually separate as they rest on different kinds of regimes.

The first section of the chapter is intended to sketch a broad panoramic view of trade in the Atlantic Basin by answering two basic questions. First, who trades with whom and by how much? Second, which Atlantic Basin trade flows have been the most dynamic in recent years? In order to simplify trade data for such a large set of countries, this first section is based on a "regional" approach that follows the classification of the WTO. In this database, the regions considered are North America (Canada, the United States, Mexico and Bermuda), Europe (including the European Union and European Free Trade Area members Iceland, Liechtenstein, Norway and Switzerland), Central and South America (including the Caribbean) and Africa (North and Sub-Saharan Africa). This classification certainly has some drawbacks, but is justified to make a very general "first cut."

Once these basic issues are established, the second section of the chapter situates Atlantic trade in a broader context in order to elucidate three further questions. First, what is the relative importance of the Atlantic Basin in relation to world trade? Second, what is the rela-

---

[1]WTO, *World Trade Developments*, WTO, *World and Regional Export Profiles*, 2008-2012; WTO, *International Trade Statistics Yearbook*, 2004. An earlier Spanish version of this chapter appeared in *Revista CIDOB d'Afers internacionals* 102/103, September 2013. That version was based on data drawn from WTO combined with data from UN Comtrade, while this one is solely based on WTO data, to make it more homogeneous. That change led to a recalculation of all the data on which the charts are based. Therefore, there are important (but not substantial) differences with the previous version in some matters.

Chart 1. Total Merchandise Inter-Regional Trade in the Atlantic Basin, 2004-2012

Million USD

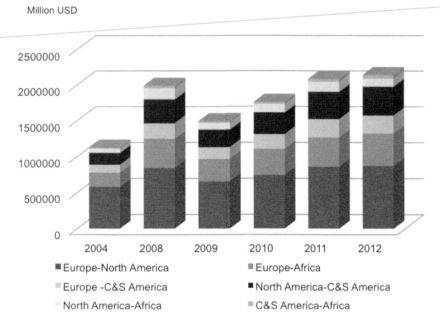

- ■ Europe-North America
- ■ Europe-Africa
- ■ Europe -C&S America
- ■ North America-C&S America
- ░ North America-Africa
- ■ C&S America-Africa

tive weight of intra-regional trade for each of the Atlantic regions? Third, given that the rise of Asia is an unavoidable dynamic in today's world trade, what is its role and influence in Atlantic trade?

The third section provides a more finely tuned analysis of some of the issues arising from the first part, notably: What is the role played by some key economies like Brazil, Mexico, Germany, Morocco, Nigeria etc. in Atlantic trade? What types of goods are traded in the Atlantic? These are important issues to be discussed as there is great variation in all these respects among and within regions. This section also enumerates some of the challenges ahead for merchandise trade in the Atlantic Basin.

Merchandise Trade in the Atlantic Basin: The Big Picture

A first look at trade data reveals that total merchandise trade within the Atlantic Basin has nearly doubled over the past eight years (Chart 1). Overall, between 2004 and 2012, total merchandise trade among

Figure 1. Distribution of Total Merchandise Trade Flows in the Atlantic Basin, 2012

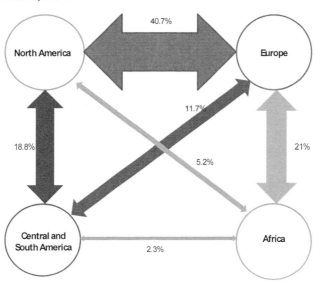

the four regions constituting the Atlantic Basin grew from $1.1 trillion to $2.14 trillion. So there is, undoubtedly a strong dynamic going on in this area of the world. This is further evidenced by the fast recovery after the 2009 crisis, which provoked a 2% drop in total Atlantic merchandise trade. Yet, by 2011, the volume of total trade had surpassed its levels of 2008.

A closer look shows that North America (itself dominated by the United States, which represents 80% of the region's exports to the world) dominates economic exchanges within the Atlantic Basin, given its strong trade relations with Europe and Central and South America (Figure 1). In 2012, these two links, with North America at its apex, represented 60% of total trade in goods in the Atlantic Basin. Merchandise trade between North America and Europe is the most important link of all, representing 40.7% of total trade in the area. This is followed by trade between Europe and Africa (21%) and between North and Central and South America (18%) which represent similar proportions. In contrast, the thinnest link is that between Central and South America and Africa, which represented only 2.3% of total merchandise trade in the Atlantic Basin in 2012. Therefore, a first conclusion is that exchange among the developed regions is the

Chart 2. Who Trades with Whom? Total Merchandise Trade Among Atlantic Basin Regions

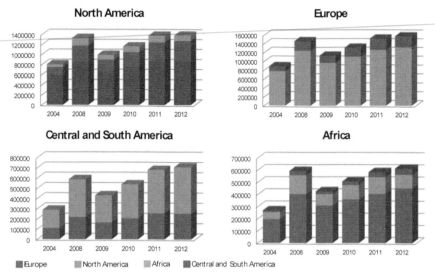

Note: All figures in million USD.
Source: Author's calculations with WTO data.

most important part of merchandise trade within the Atlantic Basin, while exchanges among the developing regions are rather marginal.

Overall Structure of Total Merchandise Trade Among Atlantic Basin Regions

It is pertinent to analyze in more detail how trade flows have been structured over the last years for each region with its Atlantic Basin partners, as the previous section suggested there is a great deal of variation in this respect. Let us examine each one in turn.

As Chart 2 and Figure 1 show, North America's most important merchandise trade partners in the Atlantic Basin are Europe (62%) and Central and South America (29%), while Africa trails far behind (8%). For the case of Europe, Chart 2 shows that North America is its most important merchandise trade partner, representing on average more than half (55%) of its total merchandise trade with the Atlantic Basin. So the high importance of the relationship between the two partners of the North Atlantic is mutual, although somewhat more important for North America than for Europe.

Also, for Europe, Africa is an important partner (28% of its total Atlantic trade in 2012), while Central and South America lags behind (16%). Thus, Europe has a more diversified merchandise trade relationship with the developing regions of the Atlantic Basin than does North America.

The data become even more interesting with regard to the developing regions of the "South Atlantic" as they mirror each other. With regard to Central and South America, Chart 2 makes its dependence on merchandise trade with North America clear: on average, exchanges with North America account for 57% of its total Atlantic merchandise trade. Europe is Central and South America's second most important merchandise trade partner in the Atlantic, representing on average 35%, while Africa trails far behind (7%).

Africa is even more dependent on its own "Northern partner": Europe on average accounted for 73% of Africa's total merchandise trade within the Atlantic Basin. North America comes second, representing 18%, and Central and South America trails with 8%. So, another important conclusion from this brief overview is that the developing regions of the Atlantic Basin, that is, Central and South America and Africa, have extremely concentrated trade relationships with their respective "Northern partners," that is, North America and Europe respectively, while they trade marginally with each other (2.3% of total Atlantic merchandise trade; see Figure 1 above).

Trends in Atlantic Basin Merchandise Trade

Having established the basic proportions of how trade flows are structured within the Atlantic Basin, it is now important to focus on trends over the last decade, for they have been influenced by strong differentials in growth across regions and other factors.

In this respect, the most striking fact is that merchandise trade in the North Atlantic (i.e. between North America and Europe) has been declining in relative importance for each of the partners over the last decade, due to sluggish growth in comparison with other regions. Europe's share of North America's total Atlantic merchandise trade has

Chart 3. Growth in Total Inter-Regional Merchandise Trade, 2004-2012 (percent)

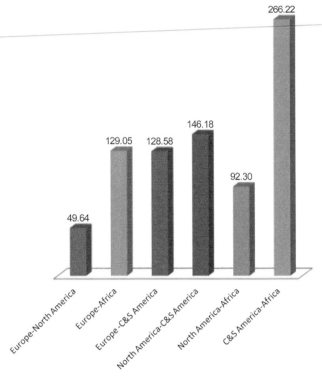

Source: Author's calculations with WTO data.

fallen from 72% in 2004 to 62% in 2011. Central and South America has taken over most of that space, as its own share has grown from 20% in 2004 to 29% in 2012, while Africa's share increased only by 1 percentage point in the same period (Chart 2). On the European side, this decline in the relative importance of North Atlantic merchandise trade has been almost identical. North America's share of Europe's Atlantic Basin merchandise trade has diminished from 65% in 2004 to 55% in 2012. This loss of 10% has been picked up by Europe's merchandise trade with faster growing (and developing) regions in Africa (from 22% to 28%) and Central and South America (from 12% to 16%).

These trends are also visible in rates of growth in total merchandise trade among dyads of regions within the Atlantic Basin. Chart 3 shows that the most dynamic links in the Atlantic Basin are the least developed ones in terms of trade volume as sketched in Chart 1 and Figure 1. Merchandise trade between Europe and North America, which is also the largest in terms of volume, was the slowest growing within the Atlantic Basin (50.6% from 2004 to 2012). This corroborates the decline of this link for both partners, relative to trade with other partners, observed above. Merchandise trade growth between North and Central and South America, which is the second largest trade link in terms of volume, was the second most dynamic (146% from 2004 to 2012).

In contrast, Africa experienced the most dynamic external merchandise trade of the four Atlantic Basin regions between 2004 and the start of the crisis, but the crisis then hit Africa badly. Africa's trade with Central and South America grew the fastest, with a 266% increase, albeit from a very low base. Such variations seem to suggest that some sort of "market maturity" is at play: trade grows fastest where opportunities have barely been explored (and existing volumes are low), while its growth is slowest where opportunities have already been exploited (and volumes are already high).

The financial crisis began in 2008; its effects on Atlantic merchandise trade links are also worth exploring, as they provide a rough indicator of vulnerability. Chart 4 indicates that the downturn of 2009 had a very important effect on merchandise trade, which dropped by 20 to 40% for all dyads in the Atlantic Basin. Africa's Atlantic merchandise trade was the most vulnerable, with a drop of nearly 40% in its exchanges with both North and Central and South America, again the smallest links in terms of volume. However, these two also bounced back fastest in the years that followed, with a new sharp drop in 2012 of trade between Africa and North America, suggesting a higher volatility in these new exchanges. In contrast, merchandise trade links in the North Atlantic (the most voluminous) were less vulnerable, dropping "only" over 20%, but they were also the slowest to recover in the years that followed, and ground to a near halt in 2012. This is not surprising, given the effects that the financial crisis has had on the economic performance and overall growth of the developed countries of the North Atlantic area, especially in Europe. Also, trade growth was already slower before the crisis hit.

Another key indicator of the structure of merchandise trade flows in the Atlantic Basin is trade balance. In that respect, Chart 5 reveals that

Chart 4. Annual Growth in Total in Total Inter-Regional Merchandise Trade, 2008-2012 (percent)

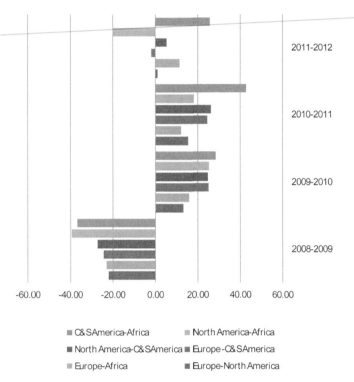

Source: Author's calculations with WTO data.

North America has a pronounced trade deficit in goods with two of its three Atlantic regional partners. This is all the more important given that it is the main hub of merchandise trade in the Atlantic, as was mentioned at the beginning of the chapter. The 2008 crisis seemed to reduce such deficits, which after a brief recovery in 2009 continued to grow, except for merchandise trade with Central and South America, with which it seems to have a stable surplus of around $30 billion. Obviously, this translates into hefty surpluses for North America's partners, especially Europe, which registers a merchandise trade surplus that averages $700 billion. In this context, any sign of protectionism or a simple fall in demand in North America is bound to have a very negative impact on Atlantic trade. Africa and Central and South America

Chart 5. Trade Balances among Atlantic Basin Regions, 2004–2012

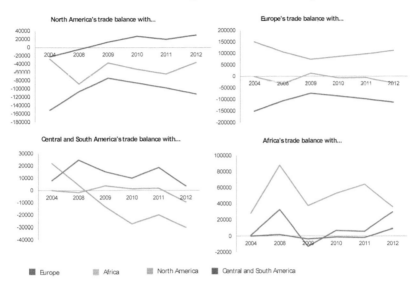

Note: All figures in million USD.
Source: Author's calculations with WTO data.

both have a merchandise trade surpluses in their trade with Europe, which reached $30 billion in 2008 and in 2011 for the latter.

The other trade links (between Africa and Central and South America, between Europe and Africa) are roughly balanced. The volumes of trade involved in these exchanges are also rather low.

The Relative Importance of Atlantic Basin Merchandise Trade

To fully understand these linkages, it is also crucial to ask how important Atlantic merchandise trade is for its regions when compared to trade with the rest of the world; to trade with other non-Atlantic regions; and to intra-regional trade. These issues are explored in this section.

The Decreasing Importance of the Atlantic Basin in World Merchandise Trade

Charts 6 and 7 clearly depict how the Atlantic Basin's share of world merchandise trade has declined over the past 50 years (all the bars below the bold black line in Chart 7). While in 1948, the Atlantic

Chart 6. Evolution of World Trade by Volume, 1953-2009

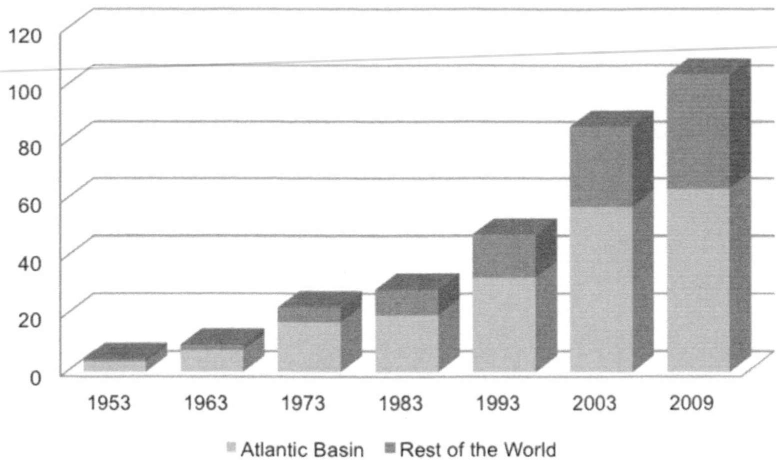

■ Atlantic Basin   ■ Rest of the World

Note: 2005 = 100
Source: Author's calculations with WTO data.

represented around 85% of the world's total merchandise trade, by 2009 it accounted for 61%. Surely, the baseline year, 1948, is rather anomalous because Europe and Asia had still not recovered from the Second World War. However, the trend is still sharply visible even if one takes the 1960s or even the 1970s as baseline, when the Atlantic still accounted for nearly 80% of world trade (77% in 1973, to be precise). It is important to note that these figures are *relative*: in absolute terms the volume of trade has been growing exponentially over the past 60 years (see Chart 6). So, although it is true that the Atlantic accounts for a diminishing share of world trade, the pie is now much bigger, and most of the world's merchandise trade is still carried out by countries situated in the Atlantic Basin.

As Chart 7 shows, the *relative* decline of the Atlantic Basin in world merchandise trade has been driven primarily by the decline of the role of the United Kingdom and the United States, as well as by Central and South America and Africa, relative to Asia's spectacular rise, which started in the 1970s, with the emergence of Japan, and then continued after the 1980s, pulled by China.[2]

---

[2]The six East Asia traders mentioned in Chart 7 are: Hong Kong, Malaysia, South Korea, Singapore, Taiwan and Thailand.

Chart 7. Share of World Trade, Key Countries and Regions, 1948–2009

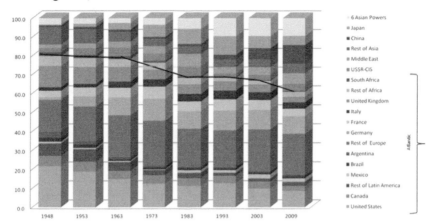

Source: Author's calculations with WTO data.

This relative decline is not even across all countries pertaining to the Atlantic Basin. The two largest economies of Latin America, Brazil and Mexico, have actually increased their share of world merchandise trade in the last four decades, albeit from a very modest basis and after many years of decline that resulted from inward-looking development strategies. Such variety calls for a more detailed analysis of particular countries, which will be carried out in the last section of this chapter.

Finally, Italy, France, Germany and the rest of Europe have managed to maintain a relatively stable share of world trade thanks to intra-European trade, which is actually quite large. The role of intra-regional trade is therefore the subject of the next section.

The Role of Intra-Regional Merchandise Trade in the Atlantic Basin

According to WTO, most trade flows take place within regions, rather than between regions. Europe has the highest level of intra-regional trade, with 71% of its merchandise exports going to other European countries (Chart 7). A large part of this is accounted for by intra-EU trade, equivalent of 65% of total EU trade.[3] This highlights the relevance of regional trade agreements, which in the case of the

---

[3]WTO, *World Trade Developments*, International Trade Statistics 2011, WTO, pp. 12-13.

Chart 8. Intra-Regional Exports as Percentage of Total Exports in 2011

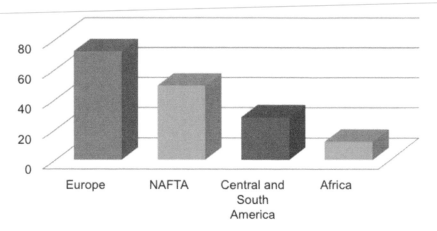

Billion USD

Source: Author's calculations with WTO data.

EU is also a customs union and a Single Market where services, capital and people also move relatively easily. In addition, the EU has an extensive free-trade agreement with EFTA, comprising the European Economic Area. To a lesser extent, the predominance of intra-regional trade also features importantly for the countries of NAFTA (North American Free Trade Area), with 49% of the member states' merchandise exports going to their partners in that region (Chart 8).

However this concentration of merchandise trade within regions is not visible for the developing partners of the Atlantic Basin. Central and South America's intra-regional exports account for 28% of the region's total merchandise exports, which is still a considerable proportion, but not so dominant as in the Northern Atlantic partners. This relative importance of intra-regional trade is probably due to the existence of several regional integration processes, the better functioning of which are the Central American Integration System (SICA, *Sistema de Integración Centro-Americano*) and MERCOSUR (*Mercado Común del Sur*). These are complemented by a number of bilateral free-trade agreements, such as the one between Chile and the MERCOSUR countries.

Chart 9. Distribution of Exports of Atlantic Basin Regions, Including Intra-Regional Trade, 2011

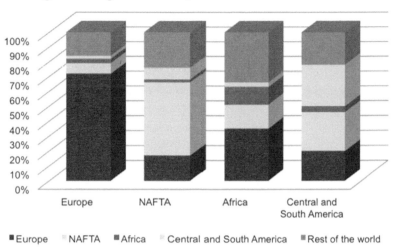

■Europe　🅔NAFTA　■Africa　🅔Central and South America　■Rest of the world

Source: Author's calculations with WTO data.

These observations about intra-regional trade become all the more important when put in the context of the Atlantic Basin and trade with the rest of the world (Chart 9). It turns out that, for European countries in particular, merchandise exports to extra-European Atlantic partners are roughly equal to their merchandise exports to the rest of the world. In terms of imports, China has displaced the United States as Europe's main supplier and, for that reason merchandise imports from the rest of the world (21%) are actually larger than those coming from extra-European Atlantic partners (12%).[4] This is very significant piece of information if we bear in mind that Europe is still the largest trader in the world, and a crucial hub of Atlantic trade. Europe does not depend as much on its merchandise trade with the Atlantic as its partners do—particularly Africa.

In stark contrast, Africa's[5] intra-regional exports only account for 12% of its total merchandise exports. It is therefore the only region in the Atlantic Basin for which intra-regional trade is not significant.

---

[4]Intra-regional trade is slightly less concentrated in imports than in exports as 66% of total imports come from other European countries.

[5]Africa includes North Africa, Sub-Saharan Africa, and South Africa.

For the case of NAFTA, intra-regional merchandise trade is also dominant, and Atlantic trade does not look as secondary as it does for Europe. Non-NAFTA Atlantic partners absorb 27% of the regions' merchandise exports, which is slightly more than NAFTA exports to the rest of the world (24%).

Central and South America is highly dependent on its Atlantic partners in terms of merchandise exports (50%), while its intra-regional trade (23%) matches its merchandise exports to the rest of the world (22% of the total). In terms of Atlantic regional partners, Central and South America exports its merchandise mainly to North America (26%) and to Europe (20%).

Africa, where intra-regional merchandise trade is lowest, is the region that depends most on Atlantic trade, with 53% of its merchandise exports going to Atlantic partners, notably Europe. Yet, it is also the most dependent on trade with the rest of the world (notably Asia), which absorbs 34% of its exports.

Asia: The Elephant in the Room?

The previous two sections have shown that to have a clearer understanding of the importance of Atlantic merchandise trade for each of its regions it is necessary to put it in perspective with regard to intra-regional trade as well as trade with the rest of the world. Within the latter category, Asia occupies a central place, given its spectacular rise in the past three decades (see Chart 7). Most of this rise has been due to East Asia, which accounted for 82% of Asia's exports in 2010, and more recently, India has joined the group of the most important players in this region.[6] It is therefore pertinent to spell out clearly its place in Atlantic trade, lest we end up avoiding addressing this "elephant in the room."

---

[6]East Asia is composed of China, Japan and the Six East Asia Traders. Unless otherwise stated, "Asia" in this paper refers to all of the region, which according to the aggregated data of the WTO classification includes the following countries: Afghanistan, Australia, Bangladesh, Bhutan, Brunei, Cambodia, China, Fiji, Hong Kong, India, Indonesia, Japan, (South) Korea, Laos, Macao, Malaysia, Maldives, Mongolia, Myanmar, Nepal, New Zealand, Pakistan, Papua New Guinea, Philippines, Samoa, Singapore, the Solomon Islands, Sri Lanka, Taiwan, Thailand, Tonga, Vanuatu, Viet Nam.

Chart 10. Total Merchandise Inter-Regional Trade of Atlantic Basin Regions Including Asia, 2004–2012

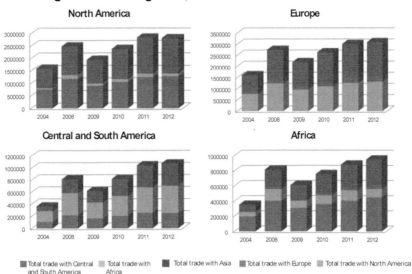

Note: All figures in million USD. Excludes intra-regional trade.
Source: Author's calculations with WTO data.

Asia's rise in world markets has been most noticed due to the flood of Chinese manufactured exports, but it must be said that the region is also a significant importer, mainly of fuels and mining products to feed its rapidly expanding industry. This is why, over the last decade, its merchandise trade has grown faster with Africa and Central and South America than with the developed regions of the North Atlantic (Chart 10). According to WTO figures, the share of Central and South American merchandise exports to Asia grew from 14% of the total in 2004 to 23% 2012, surpassing Europe (17%) as second most important destination, after North America. In terms of total merchandise, (i.e. including imports) the rise of Asia is even sharper: in 2004 it represented 27% of Central and South America's total Atlantic trade, while in 2012 this figured climbed to 52%. In the case of Africa the proportion went from 31% to 54% in the same period, with Asia overtaking North America as the second most important destination of merchandise exports.

The rise of Asia in the trade of North Atlantic partners has been slower in recent years, but it is still striking that it has also become the second largest trade partner of each of them. In the past decade, Asia has overtaken Europe and become North America's second most important trade partner, while it now matches North America in importance as Europe's main external trade partner. Actually, North America's total merchandise trade with Asia now surpasses its trade with all other Atlantic regions put together (104%), while for Europe it is getting very close to that proportion (96%) in 2012. In contrast, the South Atlantic regions still trade significantly more with other Atlantic regions put together than with Asia.

It is hard to overlook such developments as they question the very pertinence of talking about the Atlantic Basin in an isolated fashion, at least in the realm of merchandise trade. Asia has become a major trading partner with each of the Atlantic continents. And, if current trends continue in terms of trade growth, it will soon become the dominant actor in the external trade of Africa and Central and South America alike. The policy implications of this seem to be that agreements to facilitate trade in merchandise within the Atlantic are due if the basin is not to become increasingly irrelevant in the face of centrifugal forces coming from the East, especially from China and, more recently, India for the case of Africa.

Merchandise Trade in the Atlantic Basin: A Closer Look and Some Challenges Ahead

Having established the broad lines of what the "big picture" of trade in the Atlantic Basin looks like, as well as its place in world trade and its relations with Asia, it is now necessary to take a closer look at some of the individual main players, as well as to the composition of their trade, not only by destination, but also by type of product. This gives a more nuanced idea of the dynamics at play in the Atlantic Basin.

Individual Players and the Composition of their Exports and Imports

Table 1 provides a summary of the composition and destination of merchandise exports and imports of some of the Atlantic Basin's main players, as well as the rates of trade growth. A word on the selection is due here. A first cut has been to choose the largest economies for Central and South America (Argentina, Brazil) Africa (Nigeria, South

Table 1 . Major Products and Destinations of Selected Atlantic Basin Trading Countries

Country	Three major export destinations	Top 3 exports 2008-2011	Main exported goods in 2011	% of total exports	Average % yearly change in exports*	Top 3 imports	Average % yearly change in imports*
Argentina	1. Brazil	1. Oil-cake and other solid residues	Food, live animals, beverages and tobacco	37.4	0.14	1. Motor cars and vehicles	10.8
	2. China	2. Soya-bean oil and its fractions				2. Motor parts and accessories	
	3. Chile	3. Soya beans				3. Petroleum oils other than crude	
Brazil	1. China	1. Iron ores and concentrates	Inedible crude materials (except fuels)	29.6	12.4	1. Petroleum oils, crude	0.17
	2. USA	2. Petroleum oils, crude				2. Petroleum oils other than crude	
	3. Argentina	3. Soya beans				3. Motor cars and vehicles	
Mexico	1. USA	1. Petroleum oils, crude	Machinery and transport equipment	52.6	17.2	1. Petroleum oils, other than crude	16.4
	2. Canada	2. Motor cars and other motor vehicles				2. Motor parts and accessories	
	3. China	3. Reception apparatus for television				3. Electrical apparatus for line telephony	
Canada	1. USA	1. Petroleum oils, crude	Mineral fuels, lubricants and related materials	25.7	1.8	1. Motor cars and vehicles	4.3
	2. United Kingdom	2. Motor cars and other motor vehicles				2. Petroleum oils, crude	
	3. China	3. Petroleum gases				3. Parts and accessories of motor vehicles	
United States	1. Canada	1. Motor vehicles, parts and engines	Machinery and transport equipment	34.4	4.4	1. Machinery and transport equipment	3.1
	2. Mexico	2.Food and beverages				2. Mineral fuels, lubricants and related materials	
	3. China	3. Consumer goods				3. Miscellaneous manufactured articles	
Morocco	1. France	1. Diphosphorus pentaoxide	Miscellaneous manufactured articles	20.6	NA	1. Petroleum oils, crude	7.6
	2. Spain	2. Phosphoric acid				2. Petroleum oils other than crude	
	3. India	3. Wire, cable and natural calcium phosphates				3. Petroleum gases	

Table 1 (continued). Major Products and Destinations of Selected Atlantic Basin Trading Countries

Country	Three major export destinations	Top 3 exports 2008-2011	Main exported goods in 2011	% of total exports	Average % yearly change in exports*	Top 3 imports	Average % yearly change in imports*
Nigeria	1. USA	1. Petroleum oils, crude	Petroleum oils, crude	87.1	10	1. Motor cars and vehicles	17.9
	2. India	2. Petroleum oils other than crude				2. Motor vehicles for goods transport	
	3. Brazil	3. Petroleum gases				3. Motor vehicles (buses and minibuses)	
South Africa	1. China	1. Platinum	Manufactured goods classified by material (platinum)	29	9.8	1. Petroleum oils, crude	5.7
	2. USA	2. Iron ores and concentrates				2. Other unspecified commodities	
	3. Japan	3. Coal				3. Petroleum oils other than crude	
Germany	1. France	1. Machinery and transport equipment	Machinery and transport equipment	47	2.8	1. Unspecified commodities	2.8
	2. USA	2. Chemicals and related products				2. Petroleum oils, crude	
	3. Netherlands	3. Manufactured goods				3. Motor cars and vehicles designed for transport	
France	1. Germany	1. Aircraft (helicopters, airplanes...); spacecraft	Machinery and transport equipment	37.6	1.9	1. Petroleum oils, crude	3.5
	2. Italy	2. Medicaments				2. Motor cars and vehicles	
	3. Spain	3. Motor vehicles				3. Petroleum oils other than crude	
Spain	1. France	1. Motor cars and vehicles	Machinery and transport equipment	33.8	3.6	1. Motor cars and vehicles	-1.1
	2. Germany	2. Petroleum oils other than crude				2. Petroleum oils, crude	
	3. Portugal	3. Parts and accessories of motor vehicles				3. Parts and accessories of motor vehicles	
United Kingdom	1. Germany	1. Manufactured goods	Machinery and transport equipment	30.3	1.6	1. Machinery and transport equipment	8.1
	2. USA	2. Petroleum oils other than crude				2. Mineral fuels, lubricants and related materials	
	3. Netherlands	3. Chemicals				3. Miscellaneous manufactured articles	

*most recent available.

Source: United Nations, International Merchandise Trade Statistics: country profiles, 2011.

Africa) and Europe (Germany, France, the United Kingdom) and the United States, since they are the ones bound to set trends for their entire regions. Then, another group of countries has been included given their involvement in Atlantic trade, even if they are not the largest of their region (Spain, Mexico, Morocco and Canada).

A number of interesting trends are visible from this table. To start with, a look at the second column (main destination of exports) confirms for individual regional powers what was already observed for regions as a whole: the high concentration of intra-regional trade and the rising role of Asia, with China at the forefront followed by India in the case of two African countries, and Japan for one (South Africa). With the exception of African countries (which do not trade much with each other) all the other Atlantic Basin countries have at least one member of their region as major destination for their merchandise exports. This is most accentuated for European countries, where Germany and the United Kingdom have one extra-regional major partner (the United States). It is also the case for NAFTA members (Mexico and Canada) and for MERCOSUR partners (Argentina and Brazil). It seems therefore, that regional trade agreements do matter greatly in organizing exchanges.

With regard to extra-regional partners, China features in first place, as it has become a major destination of exports for five out of the ten countries studied. The United States comes second, being the major destination for the exports of four of them. Asia occupies a prominent space as destination of all three African countries, with India and Japan beside China. Another interesting observation about the destination of African exports is that there seems to be a clear division between North and Sub-Saharan Africa. While Morocco's exports go predominantly to Europe, Nigeria and South Africa trade more with Asia and the United States. This suggest that the strong dependence of Africa's exports on European markets is probably driven by North Africa's energy exports to its northern neighbors across the Mediterranean, especially when we think about Algerian and Egyptian oil and gas. In contrast, investment from Asia has grown very fast in Sub-Saharan Africa in recent years, with a corresponding rise in exports.[7]

---

[7]*The Economist*, March 23, 2013.

With regard to the composition of exports, the third column of table 1 shows a notorious North-South divide. All the developing countries of the list export mainly raw materials: oil, fuels, minerals and agricultural products. In this respect, the most extreme case is Nigeria, 87% of whose exports are constituted by crude oil, followed by other petroleum products, which makes this country a very large mono-exporter, completely vulnerable to volatile prices in oil markets. Morocco and South Africa export a more diversified list of mining products (phosphates, calcium, platinum, coal…), the value of which has been rising in the last decade, due to a very high demand in Asia. The countries of South America, Brazil and Argentina, also export raw materials, although they combine oil cake and iron ore with agricultural produce, notably soya beans and their derivatives. Argentina also has a high degree of concentration: 37% of its exports are composed of food, beverages and tobacco. According to WTO data, Central and South America's export boom has been driven by fuels and mining products as well as by agricultural products, while manufactures have lagged behind since 2007. In sharp contrast, developed countries export a much more diversified range of higher value-added products, from machinery and transport equipment to medicaments and aircraft.

The only exceptions to this pattern are located in North America. The first is Canada, which exports large quantities of petroleum crude and gas, alongside motor vehicles. The second outlier along this North-South divide is Mexico: the composition of its exports is out of line with the rest of developing countries in the list, as it is dominated by manufactures and motor vehicles, instead of raw materials, although petroleum crude is still among its major exports. With regard to destination, its major partners are not in Latin America, but its NAFTA partners, the United States and Canada. It is thus more logical to group it with North America than with the rest of Latin America, which is why, from 2003 onwards, WTO data stopped grouping it with Latin America (which is now called Central and South America) and now count it as part of North America.

With respect to imports, it is interesting to note that the North/South divide becomes less evident: all countries' imports are dominated by motor vehicles and motor parts, except for Morocco and South Africa. All of them also import petroleum products. However, developed countries import crude oil, while developing ones import refined petroleum products from the developed world. In this respect, Mexico is not different from other developing countries.

One final observation that is worth mentioning is how merchandise trade seems to be dominated by two key sectors: on the one hand, petroleum (highlighted in grey) and, on the other hand, motor vehicles and transport equipment (highlighted in brown).

Some Challenges Ahead

The main challenge ahead is that the ongoing economic crisis is provoking a new slowdown in trade. Chart 4 shows how, after two years of quick recovery following the 2009 crisis, the 2012 outlook was rather erratic. In the first two quarters of 2012, British exports fell by 4% and those of South Africa by 8%. Total EU imports from the rest of the world fell by 4.5%; this is worrisome, given the predominant place of the EU in world trade. This is largely due to a fall in GDP, and thus of demand, especially in Europe, where there is also a shortage of trade finance, prompted in particular by troubled Spanish and French banks.[8] The downturn is also now reaching Germany and even China, where the leadership is trying to shift economic focus to rising internal demand, instead of depending so much on exports.

Protectionism is another challenge to Atlantic trade. Argentina and Brazil have exhibited some of the clearest examples in recent years (automotive import restrictions in Brazil, taxes on soya exports in Argentina) while MERCOSUR's internal trade is increasingly affected by new barriers. At the multilateral level, the Doha round has stalled;[9] and it is not obvious that bilateral deals can substitute for them. EU-MERCOSUR trade negotiations stalled since the 1990s over agricultural protectionism in Europe and other issues like industrial protectionism in Brazil and Argentina, while a North Atlantic deal was abandoned in the 1990s over agriculture as well. Despite their dynamism, Africa-Central and South American trade volumes are still very low, so as to make the negotiation of a trade deal between them significant.

---

[8]*The Economist*, September 8, 2012, quoting OECD estimates.

[9]WTO members agreed to trade facilitation measures in December 2013. Although welcome, this agreement is very far from the originally ambitious Doha round.

However, not everything is lost: the EU and the United States have signed free trade agreements with Colombia, Peru and Central American countries in recent years. Mexico, Colombia, Peru and Chile also created in 2011 a Pacific Alliance, intended to liberalize the movement of goods, services and people. In 2013 the EU and Canada reached a political breakthrough regarding a comprehensive free trade agreement that could boost North Atlantic trade. This deal is important in itself, but also because it has marked a new benchmark of what "new generation" free trade agreements include: intellectual property, investment, services, government procurement and non-tariff barriers. The current negotiations for a Transatlantic Trade and Investment Partnership (TTIP) between the United States and the EU include those issues and offer an important chance for boosting trade in the Atlantic Basin.

Still, it is important to note that other key free trade initiatives are also taking place outside the Atlantic, including ongoing negotiations to create the Trans-Pacific Partnership (TPP).[10]

Conclusion

The chapter has explained that merchandise trade flows across the Atlantic Basin are organized around the United States as the main hub: the largest volume of trade takes place in the North Atlantic, and within the Americas. However, these links are growing the slowest, and were badly hit by the 2008 crisis. Developing regions (Africa and Central and South America) trade primarily with their northern developed neighbors, rather than across the Atlantic. Africa trades mainly with Europe, but its trade with the Americas is the fastest growing, especially with South America (Brazil already features as a major destination of Nigerian oil exports). Central and South America trades mainly with North America, and around one fifth of its merchandise exports go to Europe.

The chapter has also established that the relative importance of the Atlantic to its constitutive regions is variable. Europe depends least on

---

[10]The negotiating parties to the TPP are: Australia, Brunei, Canada, Chile, Japan, Malaysia, Mexico, New Zealand, Peru, Singapore, the United States, and Vietnam.

merchandise trade with Atlantic Basin partners, and decreasingly so. Yet, when intra-regional trade is taken into account, European countries depend a lot on what can still be considered as part of Atlantic trade: intra-European trade. North America offers a similar picture: the Atlantic still represents around one third of its external merchandise trade, and this share is also declining, yet if one includes intra-regional North American trade that decline is less pronounced. In contrast, the developing countries of Africa and Central and South America depend most on their extra-regional Atlantic trade, albeit they depend mainly on links with their respective "northern neighbors," and not as much on cross-Atlantic relations and intra-regional trade. Nonetheless, while South-South Atlantic merchandise trade links are both the smallest and also the most vulnerable, they are growing the fastest.

This chapter has also identified a number of trends in Atlantic merchandise trade, notably the remarkable importance of intra-regional merchandise trade (71% for Europe; 49% for NAFTA; 29% for Central and South America). This highlights that pan-Atlantic merchandise trade is less important for Atlantic countries than such trade within their own respective regions. The exception here is Africa, which is the most dependent region on Atlantic trade.

Another important trend is that, overall, the Atlantic Basin's share of world merchandise trade is decreasing: from nearly 80% at the beginning of the 1970s to over 60% in 2010. This is mainly due to the spectacular rise of Asia, and particularly of China, Japan and the Six East Asian traders. Asia seems to be "the elephant in the room" of Atlantic trade. Obviating its increasing role in the trade of all Atlantic partners poses the risk of leaving out of the analysis an important centrifugal force. Its increase in influence is felt more sharply in the developing regions: Central and South America and Africa's exports of raw materials have been boosted by Chinese demand (and Indian, in the case of Africa) in recent years. Asia has also become the largest trade partner of both Europe and North America, overtaking others in the last eight years or so.

A look at the composition and destination of merchandise exports of individual countries in the Atlantic Basin confirms the high concentration of intra-regional trade and the rising role of Asia, with China at the forefront followed by India, although the United States remains a key extra-regional partner for countries in all regions. With regard to the composition of exports, a notorious North-South divide has been identified. All the developing countries studied export mainly raw materials, while developed countries export a much more diversified range of higher value added products, like machinery and manufactures. If these countries are to sustain their economic growth and emerge from this quasi-colonial outlook in their economic relations with the world, they will need to diversify their economies and their export potential. With respect to imports in the Atlantic Basin, they are dominated by two sectors: motor vehicles and petroleum products.

Finally, merchandise trade in the Atlantic Basin faces important challenges ahead, namely sluggish economic growth due to the ongoing crisis, especially in Europe, and the threat of protectionism, which is a tempting course of action in times of hardship. With the Doha round stuck, the success of the transatlantic free-trade deal under negotiation between the United States and the EU is crucial, to prevent the "pivot towards the Pacific" from becoming irresistible to markets and governments alike. In this endeavor, the North Atlantic negotiators ought not to shut out those partners in the South which depend on trade with them so much.

Chapter 2

Commercial Ties in the Atlantic Basin: The Evolving Role of Services and Investment

Daniel S. Hamilton and Joseph P. Quinlan

Commerce in the Atlantic Basin presents a mixed picture. Commercial ties between the United States and Europe, for instance, are among the deepest and thickest in the world. U.S. and European commercial ties with South and Central America are also substantial. In contrast, the linkages between the United States and Africa, and between Latin America and Africa, while expanding, are still comparatively thin and underdeveloped. And while Europe's commercial links to Africa are significant, its relative importance is shifting as other actors appear on the scene.

Trade in merchandise goods is the primary means by which the Atlantic Basin is stitched together. These linkages are being addressed in other chapters. But regional ties are also becoming deeper via rising trade in services, greater cross-border foreign direct investment (FDI), and increasing capital flows. This chapter examines these metrics.

Services

Services are the sleeping giant of the pan-Atlantic economy. The Atlantic is home to the world's major services economies, and Atlantic economies are each other's most important services markets.[1] Global trade in services is still less important than trade in goods, since many service activities require a local presence and many countries impose restrictions on services trade. Nonetheless, services trade has intensi-

---

[1]While the services sector accounts for only 23% of global exports, it accounts for over 70% of GDP in advanced economies. Martin Wolf, *Why Globalization Works.* New Haven: Yale University Press, 2004.

25

fied and is set to expand rapidly, and Atlantic economies are poised to be major beneficiaries and drivers of the growth in global services.[2]

The United States is the largest single country trader in services, while the EU is the largest trader in services among all world regions. Most American and European jobs are in the services economy, which accounts for over 70% of U.S. and EU GDP. Over half of U.S. and EU services exports go to Atlantic Basin countries,[3] and each is seeing an increasing share of its services trade conducted with Latin America and Africa. Moreover, the delivery of services by foreign affiliates—driven by pan-Atlantic investments—has exploded over the past decade and is far more significant than services trade. The United States and EU each owe a good part of their competitive position in services globally to deep Atlantic connections in services industries provided by mutual investment flows. A good share of U.S. services exports to the world are generated by U.S. affiliates of European multinationals, just as a good share of EU services exports to the world are generated by European affiliates of U.S. multinationals.[4]

Services are not just a North Atlantic story. Services are far more important to Atlantic economies such as Brazil, South Africa, Mexico and Colombia than to non-Atlantic economies such as Russia, India or China. Brazil's expanding services industry contributes about two-thirds of its total GDP and employs about 70% of its labor force. Services account for more than 50% of GDP in Africa's 36 non-resource-rich economies and for more than 40% of GDP—more than industry's share—in the continent's resource-rich economies. As income per capita in Latin America and Africa grows, and as governments seek to diversify their economies away from commodity production, demand will grow for such services as health care, education, entertainment, insurance, telecommunications and finance. The proliferation of the internet will also induce more service-related activities in Latin America and Africa, where internet penetration remains underdeveloped. In Latin America/Caribbean, for instance, only 42.9% of the population

---

[2]The gains stemming from the liberalization of services could potentially be larger than in all other areas of international trade.

[3]Eurostat.

[4]Daniel S. Hamilton, *Europe 2020—Competitive or Complacent?* Washington, DC: Center for Transatlantic Relations, 2011.

uses the internet, while in Africa, internet usage is even lower: 15.6%. Internet penetration rates, however, in both regions are expected to rise in the years ahead owing to falling communication costs and the spread of low-cost mobile phones. Finally, services is a growing area of commercial activity among Southern Atlantic countries, particularly in energy-related services; engineering and construction services; and education and managerial services.[5]

Services have also come to dominate global foreign direct investment over the past decade, with Europe at the forefront, driving this process. Today, services represent nearly two-thirds of global FDI stock, up from a 49% share in 1990. Whereas services FDI used to be strongly related to trade and trade-supporting services for manufacturing multinationals, over the past decade more services FDI has been directed at such activities as hotels, restaurants, and financial services. Electricity, water, telecommunications and other infrastructure-related activities have also been receiving more foreign direct investment.[6]

A number of factors have lead to a rise in services FDI. The first has to do with the ascendancy of the services economy, not only in developed countries but around the world. Second, since many services are not tradable, cross-border investment is the only way to bring services to foreign customers. In addition, services FDI has expanded as more firms seek out new markets and new resources outside their home base. The dispersion of the internet and proliferation of smart phones have also helped. Finally, more Free Trade Agreements (FTAs) are centered on services, promoting greater cross-border investment in various service activities.[7]

As Figures 1 and 2 indicate, North America and the EU are highly competitive services economies and consistently record global services

---

[5]Even in resource-rich economies in Africa services between 1999 and 2008 came to account for over 40% of GDP, more than industry. See Uri Dardush and William Shaw, *Juggernaut—How Emerging Markets are Shaping Globlization.* Washington DC Carnegie Endowment for International Peace, 2012, p. 186.; http://www.economywatch.com/world_economy/brazil/structure-of-economy.html.

[6]OECD.

[7]WTO; Daniel S. Hamilton and Joseph P. Quinlan, *Globalization and Europe.* Washington, DC: Center for Transatlantic Relations, 2008, p. 75; http://trade.ec.europa.eu/doclib/docs/2010/june/tradoc_146270.pdf

Figure 1. World Total Services Trade Balance, by Region

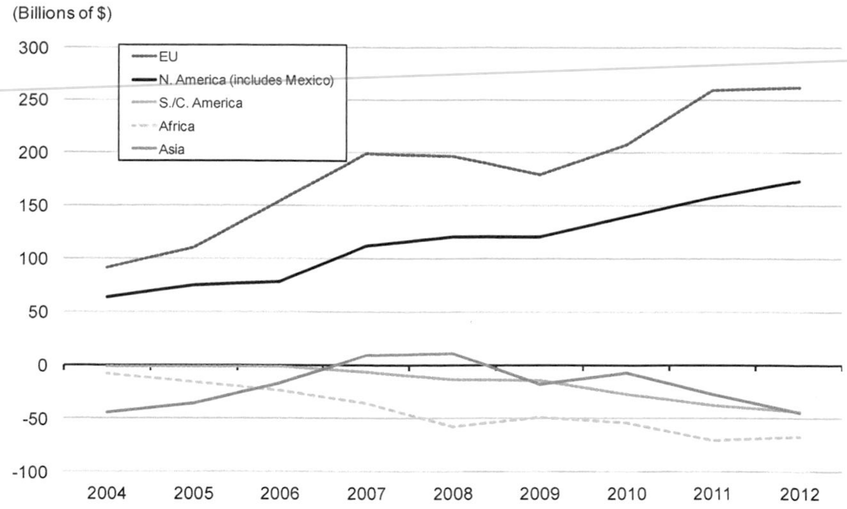

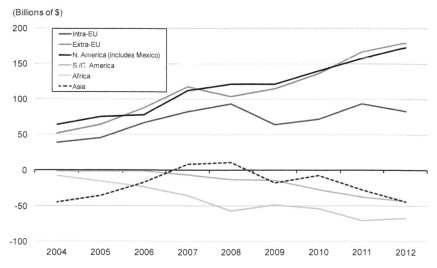

*Includes Intra-regional trade.
Source: World Trade Organization. Data as of December 2013.

Figure 2. World Total Services Trade Balance, by Region [indicating intra-regional trade]

*Includes Intra-regional trade.
Source: World Trade Organization. Data as of December 2013.

Figure 3. World Total Commercial Services Exports, by Region

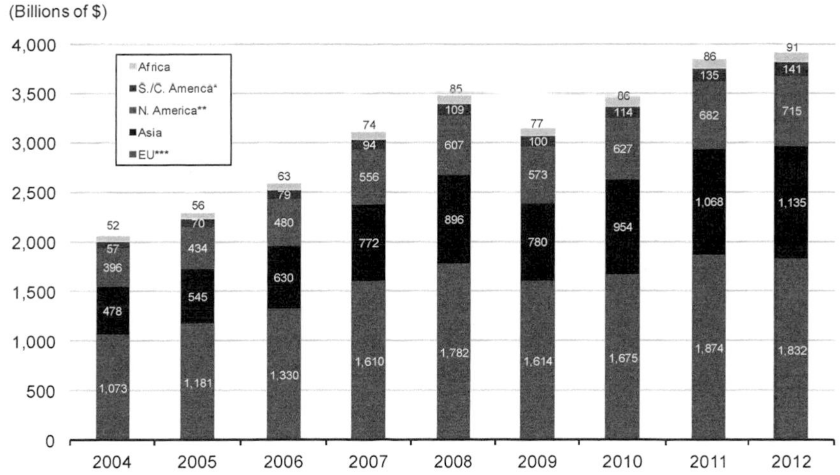

(Billions of $)

*Includes Caribbean
**U.S., Canada, and Mexico
***Includes intra-regional trade
Source: World Trade Organization. Data as of December 2013.

trade surpluses, while Asia, Africa and South and Central America each record global services trade deficits.

In 2004, EU commercial services exports were double those of Asia and North America, and in fact were more than combined commercial services exports from Asia, North America, South and Central America and Africa. In 2012 the EU still the major global commercial services exporter, although recording slightly less than double Asian exports. North America's position as a commercial services exporter, in contrast. slipped relative to Asia. However, as Figure 4 indicates, over half of EU commercial services exports re within the EU itself. The EU exports slightly fewer commercial services to the rest of the world [excluding Russia and neighboring countries] than Asia, although more than North America, South and Central America, and Africa.

In 2004, EU imports of commercial services were about twice those of Asia and almost triple those of North America. In fact, EU imports were more than combined commercial services imports of Asia, North

Figure 4. World Total Commercial Services Exports, by Region (including intra-regional exports)

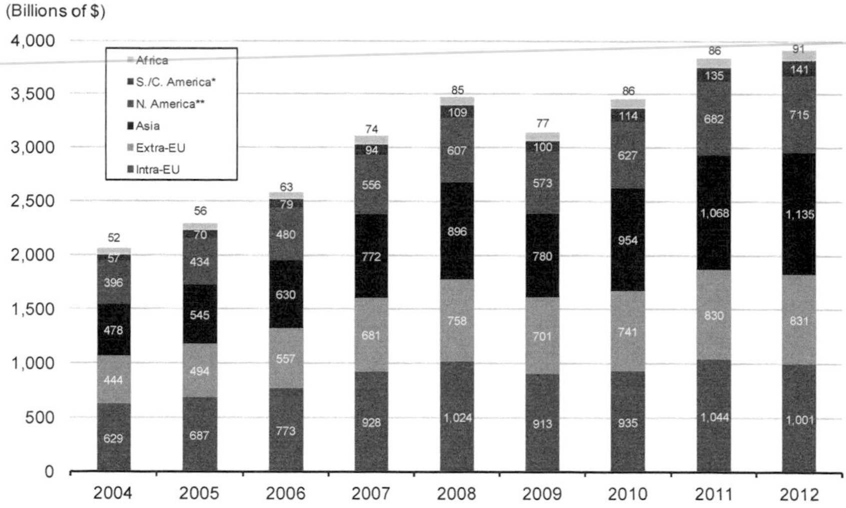

(Billions of $)

*Includes Caribbean
**U.S., Canada, and Mexico
***Includes intra-regional trade
Source: World Trade Organization. Data as of December 2013.

America, South and Central America and Africa combined. In 2012 the EU was still the largest importer of commercial services, still about triple North American imports, but Asian imports grew relative to EU imports. but now accounting for less than double Asian imports. North American, South and Central American services imports tripled, but from a low base. African imports grew more than 2.5 times over this period, but also from a low base.

However, as Figure 6 indicates, most EU commercial services imports were from other EU countries. The EU imported fewer services in 2004 from the rest of the world [excluding Russia and neighboring countries] than did Asia and about the same as North America and South and Central America combined, or North America and Africa combined.

In 2004 more than one-half of EU services exports went to North America, followed by Asia and then roughly equal shares to South and Central America and Africa. By 2012 North America was still the lead-

Figure 5. World Total Commercial Services Imports, by Region

(Billions of $)

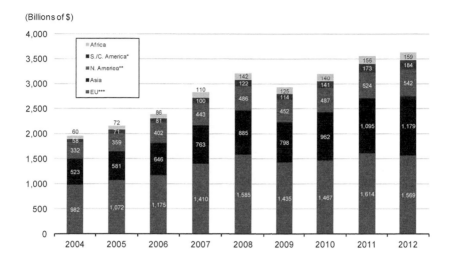

*Includes Caribbean
**U.S., Canada, and Mexico
***Includes intra-regional trade
Source: World Trade Organization. Data as of December 2013.

ing customer of EU services exports, but Asia, South and Central America and Africa had each increased its relative share of EU services exports, cutting into the North American share.

The EU registers services trade surpluses with South and Central America and Africa. It consistently registers particularly high services trade surpluses with Asia—€52.3 billion in 2012. It also registers consistent services trade surpluses with North America while recording services trade deficits with the United States, indicating that EU services trade surpluses with Canada and Mexico are relatively high.

Within the Atlantic Hemisphere, North America's share of EU services exports, while predominant, declined from 73.8% to 64.2% between 2004 and 2012. Africa's share, in contrast, rose from 12.4% to 15.9%, and South and Central America's share climbed from 13.8% to 19.9% over this period—see Figures 9 and 10.

Figure 11 indicates that in 2004 European services companies exported about 58% of their services within EU borders and only

Figure 6. World Total Commercial Services Imports, by Region (including intra-regional imports)

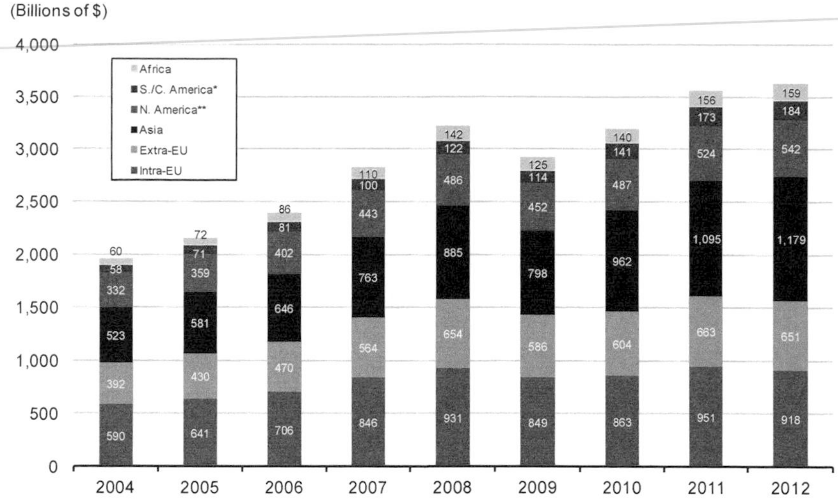

(Billions of $)

*Includes Caribbean
**U.S., Canada, and Mexico
***Includes intra-regional trade
Source: World Trade Organization. Data as of December 2013.

42% outside the EU, whereas by 2012 the intra-EU figure had fallen to just under 55% and the extra-EU demand had risen to just over 45% of total services exports. This seems to be largely explained by the enduring European recession, as the relative shift coincided with the onset of the financial crisis in 2008-2009. EU services imported from within the EU accounted for just over 60% of overall EU services imports in 2004, and had declined only slightly by 2012.

Between 2004 and 2012 U.S. services exports almost doubled, with the EU as the primary destination. The U.S. records consistent services trade surpluses with the EU and all other regions; its services trade surplus with Asia is particularly large and rising. The U.S. is particularly competitive in exports of royalties and license fees. U.S. exports of business, professional and technical services are substantial as a relative share of U.S. exports of "other private services" to all regions. Financial services exports are particularly important to Europe, educational services exports are particularly important to

Figure 7. EU Services Exports, by Region

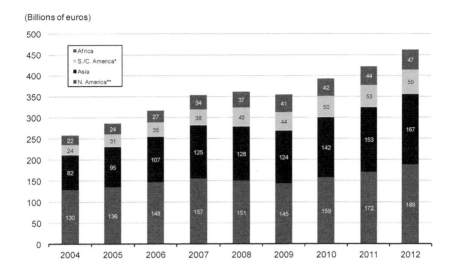

(Billions of euros)

*Includes Caribbean
**U.S., Canada, and Mexico
***Includes intra-regional trade
Source: World Trade Organization. Data as of December 2013.

Asia, and exports of telecommunications services are particularly important to South and Central America.

The EU remains the primary destination of U.S. services exports globally as well as within the Atlantic Hemisphere, although its relative share within the Hemisphere declined from 56% in 2004 to 50.3% in 2012, whereas South and Central America's share rose from 18.3% to 23.9% and the relative shares of Africa and Canada/Mexico were stagnant.

Foreign Investment Flows in the Atlantic Basin

Of the four regions of the Atlantic Hemisphere—defined here as North America, South and Central America [including Caribbean], Europe and Africa—direct foreign investment is primarily geared towards the developed markets of North America and Europe. This is to be expected—global foreign direct investment flows have a strong

Figure 8. EU Services Trade Balance, by Region

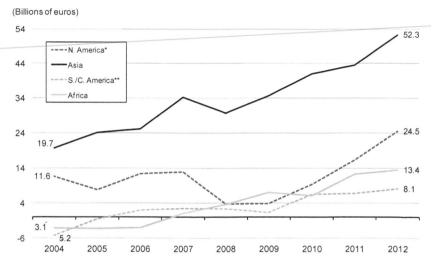

*U.S., Canada, and Mexico
**Includes Caribbean
Source: Eurostat. Data as of December 2013.

Figure 9. Percentage of EU Services Exports to Atlantic Basin, by Destination, 2004

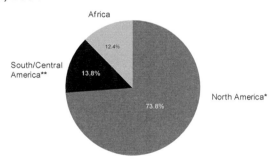

*U.S., Canada, and Mexico
**Includes Caribbean
Source: Eurostat. Data as of December 2013.

developed-nation bias given the preference of multinationals to invest in large, open, and wealthy markets that adhere and uphold strong intellectual property rights and abide by a transparent rule of law. Skilled labor is another determinant of foreign direct investment,

Figure 10. Percentage of EU Services Exports to Atlantic Basin, by Destination, 2012

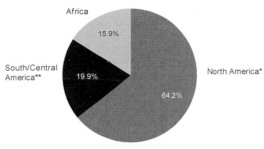

*U.S., Canada, and Mexico
**Includes Caribbean
Source: Eurostat. Data as of December 2013.

Figure 11. The Importance of Intra-EU Services Trade

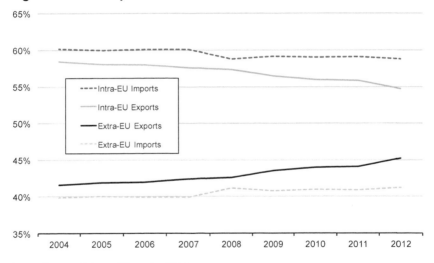

Source: Eurostat. Data as of December 2013.

which invariably means more investment between and among the United States, Canada and Europe.

As specifically outlined and discussed in our annual survey of the Transatlantic Economy,[8] the foreign direct investment ties between the

[8]See Daniel S. Hamilton and Joseph P. Quinlan, *The Transatlantic Economy 2015: Annual Survey of Jobs, Trade and Investment between the United States and Europe* (Washington, DC: Center for Transatlantic Relations, 2015), and previous editions available at http://transatlantic.sais-jhu.edu.

Figure 12. U.S. Services Exports, by Region

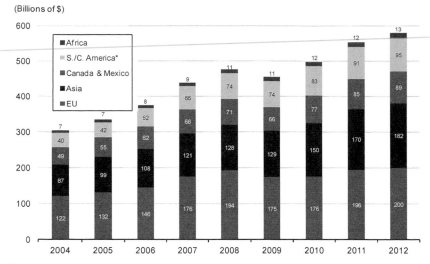

*Includes Caribbean
Source: Bureau of Economic Analysis. Data as of December 2013

United States and Europe are the deepest and thickest in the world. Hence, FDI flows in the Atlantic Hemisphere exhibit a strong North Atlantic bias. However, both South America and Africa have attracted more investment from the United States and Europe over the past decade thanks to stronger levels of growth and the rising number of middle class consumers, strengthening north-south investment ties and deepening the commercial linkages of the Atlantic Basin.

Making Room for Asian Economies

While the United States and the EU still exert a powerful influence over their partners in the Atlantic Basin, it is important to note the increasing role being played by China and India, as well as countries such as South Korea and Japan, in South and Central America and Africa. The depth and thickness of Atlantic Basin commercial ties will be influenced, if not diluted, by the growing presence of these and other non-Atlantic economies in both regions. This section briefly summarizes this dynamic.

Figure 13. U.S. Services Trade Balance, by Region

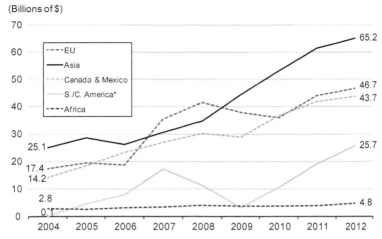

(Billions of $)

*Includes Caribbean
Source: Bureau of Economic Analysis. Data as of December 2013

For starters, whereas for decades the bulk of foreign direct investment (FDI) flowed to and from the developed nations, today a rising global share of FDI emanates from the developing nations. Global FDI increasingly bears the hallmark of global-minded corporate giants from Brazil, China, Russia and India. And where trade and investment ties, and bank lending, between these nations and Africa and South and Central America were once shallow and underdeveloped, such linkages are now thicker, more robust and more sophisticated.

A significant challenge to the notion of an integrated Atlantic Basin is this: the expanding commercial ties of two of the largest emerging economies in the world, China and India, with two of the largest emerging regions of the world, Africa and South and Central America. Commercial linkages between the various parties have soared over the past decade, but from a low base. Africa has attracted the most attention and capital of India and China relative to Latin America. Resource-seeking investment has been a prime motivator of China and India, but their investment in both Africa and South and Central America extends well beyond energy/mining. Further deepening and integration is expected in the future, challenging the stakes of the United States and Europe.

Figure 14. Percentage of U.S. Services Exports to Atlantic Basin, by Destination, 2004

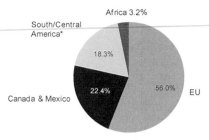

*Includes Caribbean
Source: Bureau of Economic Analysis. Data as of December 2013

Figure 15. Percentage of U.S. Services Exports to Atlantic Basin, by Destination, 2012

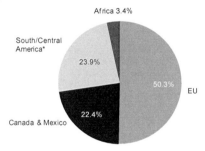

*Includes Caribbean
Source: Bureau of Economic Analysis. Data as of December 2013

In a major shift from the past, outward foreign direct investment has become an important economic dimension for both China and India. Indeed, in the past ten years, Chinese and Indian firms have become more globally-minded, with companies, motivated by market conditions and government policies, becoming more embedded in the global economy via foreign direct investment. Globally shy no more, China's outward FDI stock, totaling just $4.4 billion in 1990 (or 1.1% of GDP), spiked to $28 billion in 2000 before soaring to roughly $509 billion in 2012 (or greater than 6% of GDP). The surge reflects soaring annual FDI outflows, with outflows totaling $75 billion in 2011 and $84.2 billion in 2012; comparable levels in 2000 and 2001 were just $916 million and $6.9 billion, respectively.

Figure 16. U.S. Exports of Royalties and License Fees, 2012

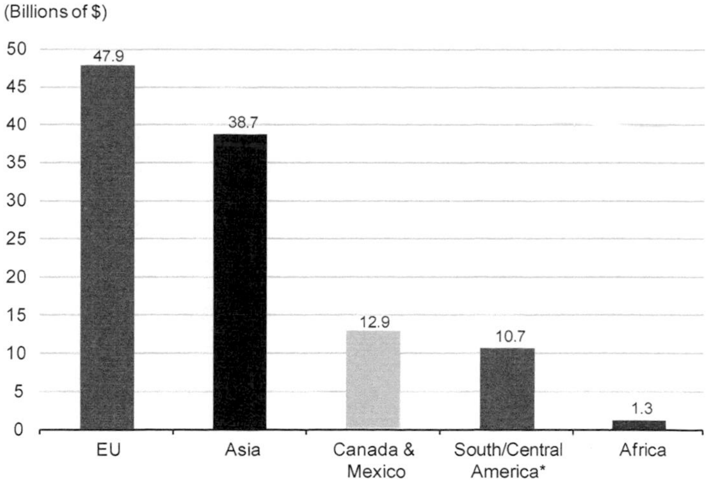

(Billions of $)

EU	47.9
Asia	38.7
Canada & Mexico	12.9
South/Central America*	10.7
Africa	1.3

*Includes Caribbean
Source: Bureau of Economic Analysis. Data as of December 2013

Outward flows from India, while not as large as China's, have been just as robust given the lower starting point. Annual FDI outflows were less than $1 billion in 2000 but peaked at $21.1 billion in 2008, prior to the financial crisis. Outflows totaled roughly $8.6 billion in 2012, pushing India's outward FDI stock to $118.2 billion in 2012, over 6% of GDP and a 68-fold increase from the beginning of the century. The combined outward FDI stock of China and India was roughly 2.7% of the global total in 2012, up from 0.4% in 2000. As of 2012, China was the 14th largest outward investor in the world, while India ranked 27th.

As Chinese and Indian firms have burrowed deeper into Africa, policymakers in the developed nations have become increasingly concerned and alarmed by the spread of China's and India's global footprint, notably in regions of the world like Africa that have long been under the West's sphere of influence. As a pointed jab at China, Secretary of State Hillary Rodham Clinton warned in a June 2011 speech in Zambia of "new colonialism" threatening the African continent.[9]

---

[9]Dambisa Moyo, "Beijing, A Boom For Africa," *The New York Times*, June 28, 2012, p. A27.

Figure 17. U.S. Other Private Services Exports, by Region, 2012

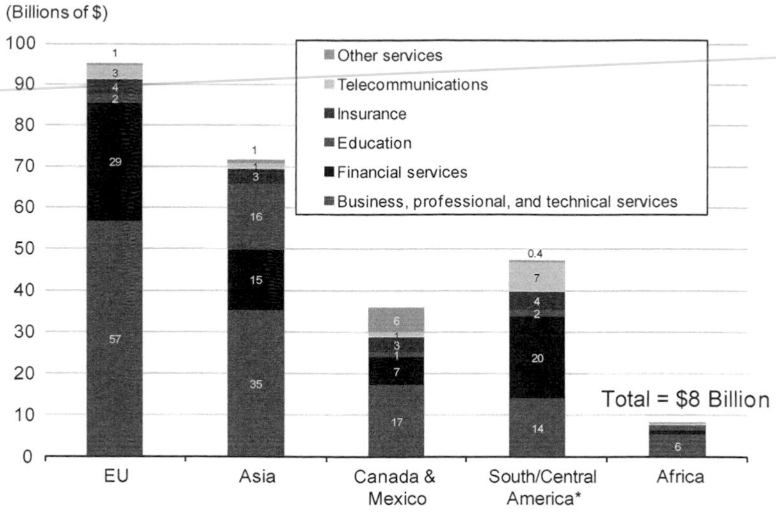

(Billions of $)

*Includes Caribbean
Source: Bureau of Economic Analysis. Data as of December 2013

Despite these worries, what is driving both nations overseas are the same variables that have long influenced and spurred U.S. and European firms to invest abroad. To this point, resource-seeking Chinese energy firms are emulating the corporate strategies of American and Japanese energy giants in the 1950s and 1960s. Where the difference lies, and where there are lingering potential areas of conflict with the United States and Europe, pivots around China's more government-led and more geo-strategic investment in Africa.

As part of China's "going out" strategy (*zou chuqu*), a key priority of Chinese foreign direct investment is securing strategic assets and natural resources to fuel the industrialization, motorization and urbanization of the Middle Kingdom. Thanks to these tectonic economic trends, China's demand for global commodities has been nothing short of stunning. The nation is now the second largest consumer of oil after the United States, and presently devours 25% of the world's soybeans, 20% of the world's corn and 16% of the world's wheat. The mainland also accounts for nearly 25% of world rubber consumption. Name the commodity and there is a good chance China is among the largest consumers in the world.

China's secular rise in commodity demand, juxtaposed against a steady decline in arable land, mounting deforestation, rising water scarcity, and herculean environmental challenges at home makes the nation fanatically focused on food and energy security for its 1.4 billion population. Hence Beijing's unstinting support to state-owned Chinese firms investing overseas in commodity-rich Africa, a strategic target of China.

There is a direct link between China's resource-seeking FDI in Africa and the nation's energy security policies. Hence, a great deal of China FDI to Africa is bundled, and includes bilateral aid and grants, low cost loans and other preferential financing arrangements provided by China's so-called policy banks—all competitive metrics that could put U.S. and European firms at a competitive disadvantage in Africa and South and Central America for that matter.

Government-led support for Chinese investment in Africa includes formal arrangements, with China launching the Forum on China-Africa Co-operation (FOCAC) in October 2000 to facilitate greater multilateral economic cooperation among key African states. This development is another way of saying that the Atlantic Basin will continue to have a strong Chinese influence. To this point, China's trade and investment with Africa has soared over the past few years. For instance, between 2000 and 2012, China's exports to Africa soared from just $4.2 billion at the start of the century to nearly $75 billion in 2012. South Africa, Nigeria and Egypt ranked as the three largest African export markets for China; South Africa alone accounted for nearly one-fifth of total exports.

Chinese imports from Africa, meanwhile, rose in comparable fashion. Imports tallied just $5.4 billion in 2000 but exceeded $105 billion in 2012; reflecting China's need for resources and China-related investment in Africa's energy infrastructure, the bulk of imports was comprised of oil and other commodities. Africa provides China with 30% of its tobacco, 25% of its pearls and precious metals, 20% of its crude oil and cocoa, 10% of its ores, and 5% of its iron and steel. Surging trade flows reflect in large part the widening presence of Chinese FDI in Africa, with the stock of outward Chinese FDI to Africa soaring from $491 million in 2003 to over $21.7 billion in 2012, more than a twenty-five fold increase.

Meanwhile, Indian FDI outflows to Africa totaled $9.3 billion over 2002-09 versus just $750 million over 1996-2002. Of the $9.3 billion total, roughly two-thirds was invested in Mauritius, a critical offshore financial center for Indian firms. Bilateral trade between India and Africa has increased dramatically over the past decade as well. Indian exports to Africa rose more than 13-fold between 2000 ($1.9 billion) and 2012 ($25 billion). Imports from Africa illustrated a similar trend, surging from $3.1 billion in 2000 to roughly $38 billion in 2012. India posted a trade deficit of $13.1 billion with Africa in 2012; China's deficit was larger—$30.8 billion.

Like Africa, Latin America has become more important to both China and India over the past decade as both as a source of raw materials and a new market for manufactured goods. China's soaring energy and agricultural needs account for China's rising investment profile in Brazil, Peru and Venezuela, the top destinations for Chinese foreign direct investment excluding the mainland's investment in the offshore centers of the Cayman Islands and the British Virgin Islands.

Latin America has been at the receiving end of many large Chinese loans to help finance natural resource-based deals and infrastructure spending. To this point, the Inter-American Dialogue notes that China loan commitments of $37 billion in 2010 were more than those from the World Bank, Inter-American Development Bank and U.S. Export-Import Bank combined.

Against this backdrop, heavy financing from Chinese banks have underwritten rising trade and investment flows between China and Latin America. In particular, the last decade has seen sharp spikes in Chinese investment in Brazil, with China's FDI stock rising from just $52 million in 2003 to $1.1 billion in 2011, Peru (from $126 million in 2003 to $802 million in 2011) and Venezuela, where China's FDI stock soared from just $19.4 million in 2003 to $802 million in 2011. As a large investor in Panama's transportation sector, Chinese FDI stock in the strategically-important nation totaled $331 million, larger than China's investment position in Mexico ($264 million).

Clearly, Chinese investment flows are ramping up, with China's investment in Latin America totaling nearly $12 billion in 2011—the largest annual increase on record, with Brazil accounting for half of the total. Indian investment has lagged behind but is expected to accelerate in the coming decade as India seeks to tap into Latin America's abundant fresh water supplies and agricultural/energy resources.

Foreign Investment in the Atlantic Basin: A Closer Look

It is the dynamic interaction between investment and trade that distinguishes the pan-Atlantic economy from all others. Foreign investment and affiliate sales power pan-Atlantic commerce and provide millions of jobs. Affiliate sales on either side of the Atlantic are more than double comparable sales in the entire Asia/Pacific.

The foreign investment picture differs for each Atlantic continent. Europe is the world's most dynamic region for FDI. The EU is the largest provider and recipient of FDI among all world regions. FDI flows have significantly deepened Europe's linkages with the rest of the world.

Patterns of Outward FDI

Despite Europe's important role as global investor, European companies invest mainly within the EU itself, underscoring the importance and attractiveness of the Single Market. In 2012 European companies invested 3.6 times as much in the EU as they did in North America and twice what they invested in the rest of the world overall. Nonetheless, EU investment in North America is substantial; at $2.437 trillion in 2012 it was about 2.6 times greater than European investment in all of Asia, 2.9 times EU investment in South and Central America and almost 10 times more than EU investment in Africa.

EU foreign direct investment in South and Central America is also considerable, totaling $851 billion in 2012, somewhat less than EU foreign direct investment in all of Asia. EU foreign direct investment in the four continents of the Atlantic Hemisphere was 3.8 times EU FDI in Asia.

North American FDI, in contrast, is directed more to the EU than to North American itself. In 2012 North American FDI in the EU was 3 times greater than North American cross-border FDI in NAFTA. North American FDI was even greater in South and Central America than in NAFTA.

Figure 18. Foreign Direct Investment Outward, 2012

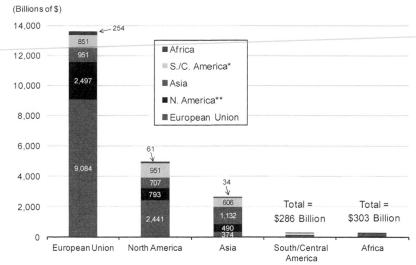

*Includes Caribbean
**U.S., Canada, and Mexico
Source: International Monetary Fund, *Coordinated Direct Investment Survey*.

North American FDI in the EU in 2012 was 3.5 times North American FDI in all of Asia and 2.6 times North American FDI in South and Central America; if non-EU countries are included the discrepancies were even higher. North American FDI in South and Central America, in turn, was greater than North American FDI in all of Asia. In total, North American FDI in the Atlantic Hemisphere was 6 times higher than North American FDI in Asia.

Most Asian FDI flows within Asia than to any individual Atlantic continent, but there is greater Asian FDI in the Atlantic Hemisphere than in the Asian Hemisphere. This reflects Asian companies seeking resources in South and Central America and Africa, and profiting from open investment regimes in North Atlantic countries. In 2012 Asian FDI in South and Central America was 18 times greater than Asian FDI in Africa. In fact, more Asian FDI flowed to South and Central America than to North America or to Europe. This reflects in part investments related to off-shore money centers in the Caribbean. Those figures are particularly noticeable when it comes to portfolio assets, but there is spillover to FDI as well.

Figure 19. South and Central America and Africa—Foreign Direct Investment Outward, 2012

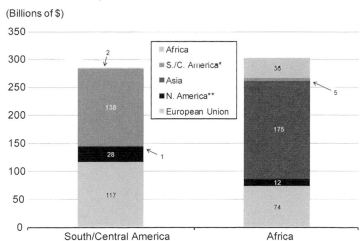

*Includes Caribbean
**U.S., Canada, and Mexico
Source: International Monetary Fund, *Coordinated Direct Investment Survey*.

Outward FDI from South and Central America and Africa in 2012 was minimal in comparison to FDI from North America, Europe or Asia. African outward FDI exceeded South and Central American outward FDI. Fifty-nine% of African outward FDI went to Asia, and 25% went to Europe in 2012—double the amount of African FDI that went to other African destinations. A plurality of outward FDI from South and Central American sources, in contrast, stayed within the region itself, with most of the rest flowing to Atlantic destinations. Asia attracted a relatively meager $1 billion in FDI from South and Central America in 2012, half the amount that flowed from South and Central America to Africa.

EU FDI in South and Central America of $537 billion in 2012 was 2.5 times North American FDI in the region of $230 billion, 8.5 times greater than Asian FDI flows to South and Central America and about 3.4 times greater than South and Central American FDI flows within the region itself.

Figure 20. Share of Atlantic Basin Total Foreign Direct Investment Outward 2012

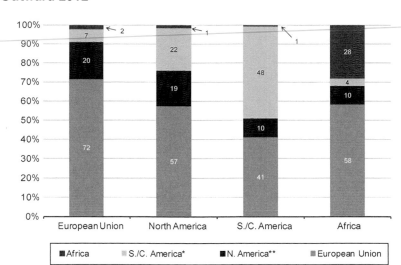

*Includes Caribbean
**U.S., Canada, and Mexico
Source: International Monetary Fund, *Coordinated Direct Investment Survey.*

EU FDI in Africa was almost 4.5 times greater than North American FDI and double Asian FDI in Africa in 2012. Asian FDI was 2.3 times North American FDI in Africa. South and Central American FDI in Africa is approaching the levels invested by North America in Africa.

Within the Atlantic Hemisphere, EU companies invested 72% within the EU itself in 2012. Fifty-seven% of North American FDI within the Atlantic Hemisphere, in contrast, flowed to the EU, and 22% to South and Central America, compared to just 19% within NAFTA itself, and only 2% to Africa. Forty-eight percent of South and Central American FDI within the Atlantic Hemisphere stayed within the region itself, followed closely by flows to the EU; only 10% flowed to North America and only 1% to Africa. Fifty-eight percent of African FDI within the Atlantic Hemisphere flowed to the EU, more than double African FDI within Africa itself. North America accounted for 10% and South and Central America for only 4% of African FDI within the Atlantic Hemisphere.

Figure 21. Foreign Direct Investment Inward 2012

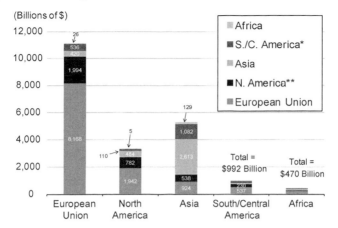

*Includes Caribbean
**U.S., Canada, and Mexico
Source: International Monetary Fund, Coordinated Direct Investment Survey.

Patterns of Inward FDI

Most FDI in the EU comes from European companies themselves. Inner-EU FDI in 2012 was four times the level of North American investment in the EU. Yet North American FDI of $2 trillion was about 2.3 times more than South and Central American FDI in the EU and almost 5 times the level of Asian FDI in the EU.

The United States is by far the most important source country of foreign direct investment in the European Union. Despite the rise of other markets, Europe continues to account for 56% of U.S. foreign direct investment worldwide. U.S. investment in Europe is nearly four times larger than U.S. investment in all of Asia and 13 times more than U.S. investment in the BRICs. Between 2000 and 2012 China accounted for only about 1% of total global U.S. investment, less than tiny Belgium. U.S. investment in the Netherlands during this period was more than 14 times larger than in China. And in 2011 and 2012 U.S. companies have actually disinvested $6.5 billion from China while investing $428 billion in Europe. U.S. affiliate income from China and India together in 2011 ($13.1 billion) was less than half U.S. affiliate earnings in Ireland ($29 billion).

Announcements in 2010 of new investments by Chinese companies in Greece attracted considerable attention and anticipation of surging Chinese investments in Europe. Such investments can of course be important for Greek ports and shipping, but overall the volume of Chinese investment in Europe is quite low.[10] In fact, for all the talk of Asian investment in Europe, total Asian FDI in the EU in 2012 was significantly less than South and Central American FDI in the EU. FDI from non-EU Atlantic Hemisphere sources in 2012 were 6 times Asian FDI in the EU.

The EU is the largest source of FDI in North America; EU FDI in North America in 2012 was about 2.5 times North American FDI within the region itself and 4 times the level of Asian FDI in North America. EU investment in the United States accounts for 74% of total foreign direct investment in the U.S. and is 27 times the level of EU investment in China and more than 55 times the level of EU investment in India. In fact, there is more European investment in a single U.S. state such as Indiana or Georgia than all U.S. investment in China, Japan and India combined.

Most FDI within Asia comes from Asian countries themselves. The second largest source of FDI in Asia, however, is South and Central America, which in 2012 accounted for 41% of inner-Asian FDI in Asia, more than EU FDI in Asia and double North American FDI in Asia. This is largely due to flows from Caribbean money centers and is most likely Asian investments that are repatriated back to Asia.

A variety of factors limit North American and European FDI in Asia. Many negative considerations dampening such flows are specific to individual countries. For example, inefficient bureaucracy and a poorly developed infrastructure figure among the most important barriers for FDI in India. In China, investor concerns about property rights, intellectual property and remaining restrictions and caps on foreign ownership in the service sectors limit EU and North American investment.[11]

---

[10]European Competitiveness Report 2009.

[11]M. Frenkel, K. Funke and G. Stadtmann, "A Panel Analysis of Bilateral FDI Flows to Emerging Economies," *Economic Systems*, Vol. 28, (2004), pp. 281-300; Gábor Hunya, "Austrian FDI by Main Countries and Industries," FIW Study No. 015 (2008); Hunya and Stöllinger, op. cit.; D. Bartlett, "Economic Trends in the BRIC Countries," April 7, 2008, http://www.the-financedirector.com/features/feature1710/.

Figure 22. South and Central America and Africa Foreign Direct Investment Inward, 2012

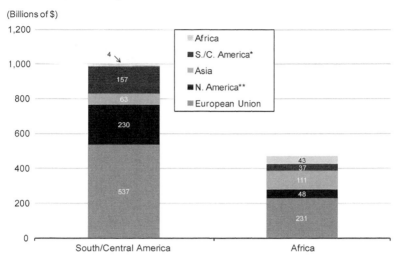

*Includes Caribbean
**U.S., Canada, and Mexico
Source: International Monetary Fund, *Coordinated Direct Investment Survey.*

The EU is the largest source of FDI in South and Central America, accounting for 2.3 times the level of North American investment in the region in 2012. The eurozone accounts for 40% of all FDI in Latin America, the EU is the biggest foreign investor in Brazil, and São Paulo hosts the largest concentration of German corporate investment outside Germany. Since 2000, U.S. and European firms have each invested significantly more capital in Brazil than in China. Both EU and North American FDI in the region is greater than intra-regional FDI, which in 2012 accounted for only 29% of EU FDI and 68% of North American FDI in the region.

The EU is the largest source of FDI in Africa, accounting for twice Asian FDI in Africa and 5 times more than North American FDI in Africa in 2012. The EU, Asia and North America all invested more in Africa than African companies invested in Africa.

FDI ties between South and Central America and Africa are weak. South and Central America invested $37 billion in Africa in 2012, and Africa invested only $2 billion in South and Central America.

Figure 23. Share of Atlantic Basin Total Foreign Direct Investment Inward 2012

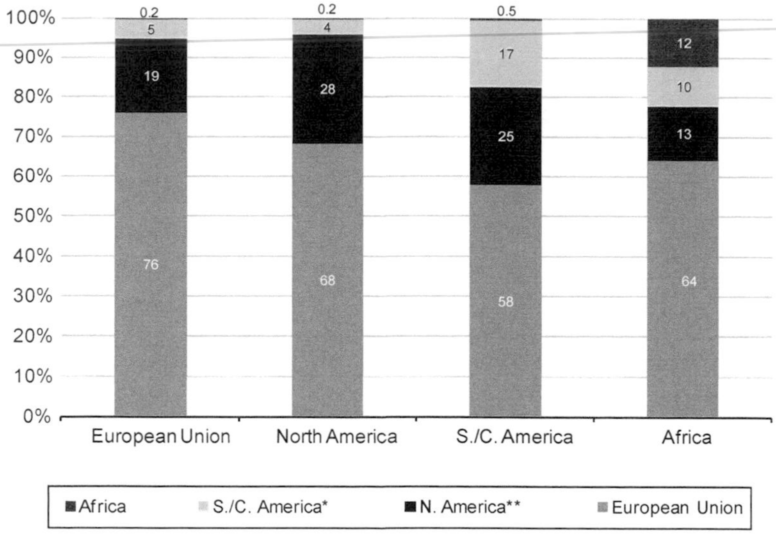

*Includes Caribbean
**U.S., Canada, and Mexico
Source: International Monetary Fund, Coordinated Direct Investment Survey.

Portfolio Investments[12]

In 1900, private capital flows could be measured in the hundreds of millions of dollars, and involved relatively few countries.[13] Today, they are measured in the hundreds of billions of dollars, and many, many countries are involved. Money is traded around the clock, with more and more of the world's financial markets electronically connected and linked.

---

[12]Portfolio investment includes equity securities such as shares, stocks, and mutual funds; and debt securities such as bonds, Treasury bills and commercial and finance paper.

[13]For an overview of capital flows then and now, see Lund and Roxburgh, *op. cit.*; Michael Bordo, "Globalization in Historical Perspective," *Business Economics*, January 2002; Kevin H. O'Rourke and Jeffrey G. Williamson, *Globalization and History: The Evolution of a Nineteenth-Century Atlantic Economy* (Cambridge, MA: MIT Press, 1999); Michael D. Bordo, Barry Eichengreen and Douglas A. Irwin, "Is Globalization Today Really Different from Globalization a Hundred Years Ago?" in Susan M. Collins and Robert Z. Lawrence, *Brookings Trade Forum 1999* (Washington, DC: Brookings Institution Press, 1999)

Most investment during those early days of globalization was limited largely to portfolio investment in railroads, municipal and national bonds, and a few other types of assets in the newly emerging markets of the time. Lending focused on governmental authorities. Foreign direct investment played a smaller role, and production processes were not as highly integrated as they are now. In recent decades, however, the breadth and depth of international capital investments grew rapidly. Firms used their investments to form alliances and extend value chains internationally in very complex networks. Industry, finance, and the services sector in emerging markets became important candidates for foreign portfolio investments.

The result was a significant boost in capital flows around the world. From 1980 through 2007, the world's financial assets—including equities, private and public debt, and bank deposits—nearly quadrupled in size relative to global GDP. Global capital flows similarly surged. Between 1990 and 2006, cross-border capital flows grew more than 10% annually. Over this period, capital flows to emerging markets grew twice as fast as inflows to developed countries.[14] In the wake of the Great Recession, as the EU, the U.S. and Japan record low growth and struggle with debt and challenges to their still-fragile financial systems, the flow of capital to emerging markets has accelerated, prompting some capitals to adopt controls on the inflow.

Daily turnover in the foreign exchange markets totaled $3.2 trillion on the eve of the recession in early 2007, an increase of over 70% from 2004 and nearly four times that of two decades earlier. The dollar and the euro were at the cutting edge of this trend, accounting for most daily global turnover. The velocity of capital also spawned more of a global equity culture, evident by the fact that at the end of 2006, the world's stock market capitalization represented 99.2% of world output, up from a 36.2% share in 1990.

At the same time, however, credit bubbles grew both in the United States and Europe. Contrary to popular perceptions, credit in Europe grew larger as a% of GDP than in the United States. Total U.S. credit outstanding rose from 221% of GDP in 2000 to 291% in 2008, reaching $42 trillion. Eurozone indebtedness rose even higher, to 304% of

---

[14]Much of this section is drawn from Lund and Roxburgh, *op.cit.*

Figure 24. Regional Composition of Portfolio Assets, 2012

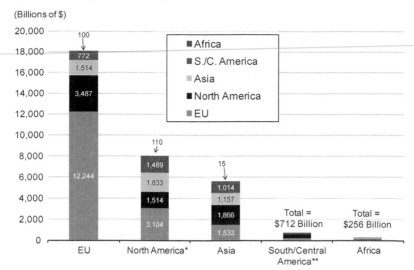

*U.S., Canada, and Mexico
**Includes Caribbean
Source: International Monetary Fund, *Coordinated Portfolio Investment Survey.*

GDP by the end of 2008, while UK borrowing climbed even higher, to 320%.[15]

Finally, the bubble burst. The global economic crisis was triggered by the deteriorating quality of U.S. subprime mortgages—housing loans offered to homebuyers at below prime rates. Although this device was invented and offered widely in the United States, these mortgages were packaged or securitized, then given top-rate credit ratings, and sold all over the world. Many European banks and investors snapped up these mortgage-related instruments, such as collateralized debt obligations, credit default swaps and structured investment vehicles (SIVs). In addition, many European banks were eager lenders to construction firms and households, given low global interest rates and abundant levels of global capital. When falling home prices and a series of defaults turned into a major subprime meltdown in the U.S. in 2007, Europe was also engulfed in a global credit crisis.

---

[15]Lund and Roxburgh, *op. cit.*

Figure 25. Regional Composition of EU Portfolio Assets, 2012

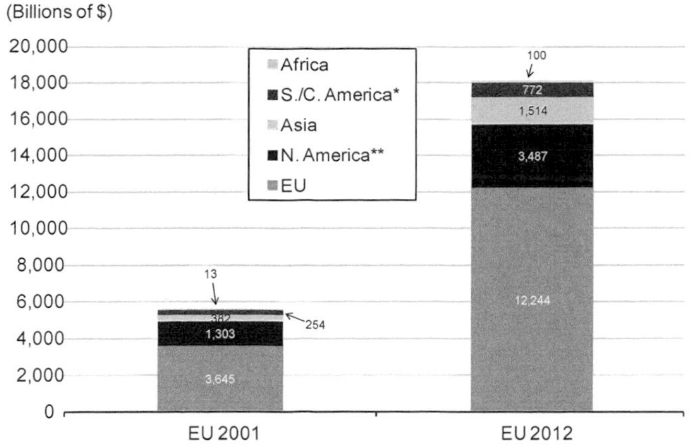

(Billions of $)

■ Africa		
■ S./C. America*		
■ Asia		
■ N. America**		
■ EU		

EU 2001 values: 13, 362, 1,303, 254, 3,645

EU 2012 values: 100, 772, 1,514, 3,487, 12,244

*Includes Caribbean
**U.S., Canada, and Mexico
Source: International Monetary Fund, *Coordinated Portfolio Investment Survey.*

The global financial crisis and worldwide recession abruptly halted nearly three decades of expansion for international capital markets. It has raised widespread concerns about the volatility of capital flows and generated a greater sense of vulnerability among stakeholders to such flows. The total value of the world's financial assets fell by $16 trillion in 2008, to $178 trillion, the largest setback on record.[16] Declines in equity and real estate wiped out $28.8 trillion of global wealth in 2008 and the first half of 2009. Cross-border capital flows[17] fell 82% from $10.5 trillion in 2007 to just $1.9 trillion in 2008. Relative to GDP, the 2008 level of cross-border capital flows was the lowest since 1991. Cross-border lending fell from $4.9 trillion in 2007 to minus $1.3 trillion in 2008, meaning that lenders cancelled more cross-border loans than they made. In the worst-hit countries, foreign bank credit contracted by as much as 67%. Flows of foreign deposits also reversed course, as investors withdrew $400 billion of deposits from foreign financial centers in 2008.[18]

---

[16]By 2007, the total value of global financial assets reached a peak of $194 trillion, equal to 343% of GDP. See Hamilton and Quinlan, *The Transatlantic Economy 2010*, op. cit.

[17]This includes foreign direct investment (FDI), purchases and sales of foreign equities and debt securities, and cross-border lending and deposits.

[18]Lund and Roxburgh, *op. cit.*

Figure 26. Regional Composition of North America Portfolio Assets, 2012

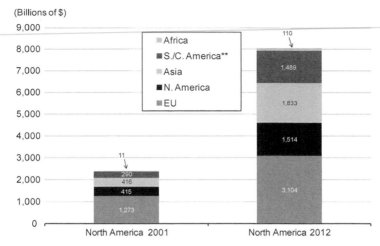

*U.S., Canada, and Mexico
**Includes Caribbean
Source: International Monetary Fund, *Coordinated Portfolio Investment Survey.*

Across world regions, the UK and the eurozone experienced the largest declines in cross-border capital flows. In 2008 foreign investors withdrew more money from the UK than they put in. The fall-off in capital flows in western Europe— equivalent to 21% of collective GDP—reflected the reversal of lending flows between the UK and the eurozone, a decline in flows between individual eurozone countries, and the plunge of flows between European countries and the United States.

The financial crisis and attendant recession has had a powerful impact especially among North Atlantic countries. Financial markets in Europe and North America have been stagnant or grown slowly while fiscal deficits have cause government debt to soar. Capital flows are slowly reviving and developing new patterns.[19] Many emerging

---

[19]According to the McKinsey Global Institute, "2008 may have marked an inflection point in the growth trajectory of financial markets in North America, Europe, and Japan. Financial assets in those regions more than tripled from 1990 through 2007, to $158 trillion, or 403 percent of GDP. But the circumstances that fueled the rapid increases of past years, particularly in equities and private debt, have changed, making it likely that total financial assets will grow more in line with GDP in coming years." Ibid.

Figure 27. Regional Composition of South/Central America and Africa Portfolio Assets, 2012

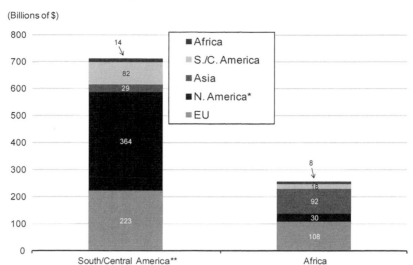

(Billions of $)

*U.S., Canada, and Mexico
**Includes Caribbean
Source: International Monetary Fund, *Coordinated Portfolio Investment Survey.*

markets have suffered as well, while others have advanced. Yet overall developing nations—despite having over $10 trillion at their disposal in the form of international reserves—have failed to effectively use their financial firepower to stave off a cyclical economic slowdown, let alone marshal their massive savings to fundamentally remake the global financial order. Fears that the U.S. Federal Reserve would "taper," or gradually remove, excess liquidity from the U.S. capital markets, sparked a firestorm in the emerging markets in 2013, prompting massive capital outflows in many developing nations and attendant macroeconomic problems for nations like South Africa, Brazil, Russia, Turkey and many others. These trends were a strong reminder that the developed nations still largely dictate and influence global capital flows, and remain at the center of the global financial universe.

Nonetheless beyond the headlines the global financial architecture is being reconfigured, and various crosscurrents are at work. Overall, for investors and financial intermediaries alike, emerging markets will become more important as their share of global capital markets continues to expand.[20] The question for this chapter is how such shifting patterns may play out across the Atlantic Basin. A number of charts can illuminate the current nature of and relationships among portfolio assets.

Figure 24 indicates that in 2012 total portfolio assets in the EU were significantly more than those in North America and in Asia. The EU was the largest holder of portfolio assets in North America, while North America was the largest holder of portfolio assets in Asia.

Portfolio assets in the EU grew from $5.597 trillion in 2001 to $18.117 trillion in 2012. EU portfolio holders account for about two-thirds of those assets. North America accounted for $3.487 trillion and Asia for $1.514 trillion; South and Central American and African portfolio assets in the EU grew rapidly from 2001, but each from a low base.

Portfolio assets in North America grew from $2.405 trillion in 2001 to $8.050 trillion in 2012. The EU held triple the value of North American portfolio assets than North Americans held of each other's assets in 2001, and about double in 2012. Asia's share was roughly equal to North America's own share in 2001; by 2012 Asia's share had grown relative to North America's share. South and Central American portfolio assets in North America grew rapidly from 2001 to roughly equal North American cross-border portfolio assets in North America. Africa's assets in North America grew rapidly over this period, but from a low base.

North America increased its portfolio holdings in South and Central America four-fold between 2001 and 2011, accounting for over half of the region's assets. The EU was the only other major asset holder. The region's own holdings are modest, and both Asia and Africa are non-players.

In contrast, Asia and the EU were roughly equal as portfolio asset holders in Africa, each accounting for roughly 3 times greater assets than North America held in Africa. The trend is also quite striking. Whereas in 2001 Asian portfolio assets in Africa were practically non-existent, they have risen dramatically. EU portfolio assets in Africa also

---

[20]Ibid.

Figure 28. Portfolio Investment, Total Assets, 2001/2012

Portfolio Investment, Total Assets, 2012									
	Investment From (Billions of $)...								
	EU		North America		Asia		South/Central America		Africa	
Investment In...	$	% Total	$	% Total	$	% Total	$	% Total	$	% Total
EU	12,244	61.8%	3,104	35.1%	1,533	24.8%	223.0	29.7%	108	40.7%
North America*	3,487	17.6%	1,514	17.1%	1,866	30.2%	364	48.4%	30	11.4%
Asia	1,514	7.6%	1,833	20.7%	1,157	18.7%	29	3.9%	92	34.9%
South/Central America**	772	3.9%	1,489	16.8%	1,014	16.4%	82	10.9%	18	6.7%
Africa	100	0.5%	110	1.2%	15	0.3%	14	1.9%	8	2.9%
World Total	19,823	91.4%	8,841	91.1%	6,179	90.4%	752	94.8%	264	96.7%

Portfolio Investment, Total Assets, 2001									
	Investment From (Billions of $)...								
	EU		North America		Asia		South/Central America		Africa	
Investment In...	$	% Total	$	% Total	$	% Total	$	% Total	$	% Total
EU	3,645	60.6%	1,273	49.6%	614	35.7%	36.2	12.8%	23	71.8%
North America*	1,303	21.6%	415	16.2%	642	37.4%	193	68.3%	5	15.8%
Asia	382	6.3%	416	16.2%	152	8.9%	9	3.1%	1	3.1%
South/Central America**	254	4.2%	290	11.3%	210	12.2%	39	13.7%	0.3	0.9%
Africa	13	0.2%	11	0.4%	2	0.1%	2	0.7%	0.1	0.2%
World Total	6,019	93.0%	2,565	93.8%	1,719	94.3%	283	98.5%	32	91.8%

*Includes Caribbean
**U.S., Canada, and Mexico
Source: International Monetary Fund, Coordinated Portfolio Investment Survey.

rose 4 times in this period, but in 2001 the EU accounted for the vast majority of African portfolio assets, now its share is roughly equal to that of Asia. South and Central American portfolio assets in Africa have also grown to about half of North American assets held in Africa

Between 2001 and 2012 the EU's share of total portfolio assets in Africa fell from 71.8% to 40.7%, and North America's share fell from 15.8% to 11.4%. The Atlantic Hemisphere's share overall in Africa fell from 88.7% in 2001 to 61.8% in 2012, reflecting the ascendancy of Asia in Africa.

In South and Central America North America's share of total portfolio assets fell from 68.3% to 48.4% , while the EU's share rose from 12.8% to 29.7%. South and Central American holdings also declined from a 13.7% share in 2001 to a 10.9% share in 2012. Africa remained a non-player; Asia's investment share was also marginal.

In the EU the region's own share of portfolio assets remained high and steady at 61.8% in 2012, whereas North America's share fell from 21.6% in 2001 to 17.6% in 2012, although the Atlantic Hemisphere's share of EU portfolio assets remained high at 83.8%.

In North America, in contrast, the Atlantic Hemisphere's share fell from 77.5% in 2001 to 70.2% in 2012. The EU's share fell from 49.6% in 2001 to 35.1% in 2012, while South and Central America's share rose from 11.3% in 2001 to 16.8% in 2012. Asia's share also increased from 16.2% to 20.7%.

Chapter 3

Harmonized Trade Preferences for Low-Income African Countries: A Pan-Atlantic Initiative

Eveline Herfkens

Sub-Saharan Africa (SSA) needs to expand exports in order to create jobs, raise incomes, and, ultimately, reduce poverty and aid dependency. Domestic markets in most SSA countries are simply too small to enable local industry to achieve economies of scale. Increased trade opportunities would encourage both domestic and foreign investment that is critical to long term balanced development.

The region's exports have been growing rapidly, about 14% per annum in the last decade. But the bulk of the growth has come from increased exports of oil and raw materials. The important emergence of value chains virtually by-passed the region: by 2010 SSA had lower ratios of parts and components in their imports than in 1980.[1] And its overall share of world trade is a miniscule 2.2%. This marginalization of the region is critical in holding back its development.

In order to for SSA to improve its capacity to exploit trade opportunities and diversify its economies many obstacles have to be tackled: the lack of one common regional market to reduce "internal" trade costs first and foremost.[2] And much remains to be done regarding the domestic supply side: investment is needed in reliable energy supply; in infrastructure to reduce transport costs; in human capital and institutional capacity; and in general in improving the investment and business environment. Transaction costs for trade, reducing international competiveness, are high: the time to export for the region is 37 days, while the world average is 25 days; the cost per container is $1,942, compared to the world average of $1,390.[3] All of these issues

---

[1]Michalopoulos, C. and F. Ng, "Trends in Developing Country Trade, 1980-2011" *Policy Research Working Paper*, No. 6334. Washington, DC: World Bank, 2013.

[2]Collier, P. and A. Venables, "*Rethinking Trade Preferences to Help Diversify African Exports,*" CEPR Policy Insight No. 2, June 2007.

[3]World Bank, *Doing Business 2013*, http://www.doingbusiness.org/special-features/infograph.

are the responsibility of African governments themselves (though foreign aid can help).

Africa's improved trade and economic performance over the last decade shows that many of these issues are in fact being addressed. Over the past eight years 45 of 46 Sub-Saharan governments improved their economies' regulatory environment for business—with an average of nine institutional and regulatory reforms per economy.[4]

But more can also be done to improve the external environment. This chapter focuses on this dimension of trade: access to developed and emerging world markets.

Trade policies around the world discriminate against the manufacturing and agricultural exports of poor countries. Average tariffs in rich countries are in the low single digits, but tariffs are still high in sectors where poor countries do well. This is supposedly being addressed by preferential schemes offered by the OECD and some emerging economies that provide special access for exports from the least developed countries (LDCs),[5] or, in the case of the United States, from Sub-Saharan Africa. But the utilization of the European scheme has been quite limited, and in the case of the U.S. scheme relevant products are excluded and those countries that need preferences most have not benefitted significantly from them.

In the meantime, while the Doha Round of global trade negotiations has collapsed, bilateral and regional free trade agreements (FTAs) have proliferated. Such agreements discriminate against non-participants, as they may divert trade from cheaper non-member sources to more expensive member sources. And they often force joining developing countries to take on onerous commitments—beyond those they have agreed in the WTO—in areas such as intellectual property rights while trade-distorting subsidies used by developed countries in areas such as agriculture are not addressed.[6] Thus, small and poor countries tend to lose out, while their preferential margins

---

[4]Ibid.

[5]These are the 49 countries that meet the UN criteria involving per capita income, industrial and human development indices; 27 of these are in Sub-Sahara Africa.

[6]Nkomo, M., "The Under-Utilization of TRIPS Flexibilities by Developing Countries: The Case of Africa," in WTO-WIPO, *Colloquium for Teachers of Intellectual Property*, Geneva: WTO, 2011.

erode, as overall levels of protection are reduced. This hurts African exports, including in sectors that have developed recently, benefitting from present schemes, however imperfect, such as the textile and apparel industries that target the U.S. market through the African Growth and Opportunity Act (AGOA). While the current initiative for a new Transatlantic Trade and Investment Partnership (TTIP) can be a promising boost for the European and U.S. economies, it would leave Sub-Sahara Africa out in the cold.

Enhanced trade preferences for Sub-Sahara Africa are needed in order to spur investment in labor intensive export sectors and processes that offer opportunities for increased employment. The region simply has to diversify its production base away from heavy reliance on primary commodities.

Preference schemes need to focus on full utilization by low-income and lower-middle-income countries that are able to benefit from such schemes. They also need to cover all products, and particularly those in which these countries have a comparative advantage (agriculture and labor-intensive manufacturing products, including apparel and footwear); their rules (particularly the rules of origin, below) need to be simple, allow cumulation with regional partners and flexible for beneficiaries to be able to use the schemes; and they need to be stable and predictable in order to attract investment.

This chapter proposes to give priority to not just minimizing further erosion of Sub-Saharan market access, but to improve, harmonize and modernize present schemes by establishing one common and generous system of trade preferences for low and lower middle income Sub-Saharan African country exports into European and North American (including Canada) markets. It also suggests, given the importance of emerging markets for Sub-Saharan exports, and building on preferences already given by some countries in Latin America to the Least Developed Countries (LDCs), to make this a truly Atlantic-wide effort, by inviting Latin America to join in offering the same market access.

Trade Preferences Relevant to Sub-Saharan Africa

At present there are several different preferential trade arrangements in favor of low-income and least-developed countries in Africa. The EU, the United States, Canada and Brazil all have separate and different preferential trade arrangements, with different country and product coverage and different requirements regarding the rules of origin that permit goods to qualify for preferential treatment (See Annex for details of each scheme).[7] The complexity of these diverse arrangements presents serious challenges for countries in Africa with limited institutional capacity. As a consequence, their utilization of these trade preferences is limited and the benefits they derive are much less than they could be.

U.S. Scheme: The African Growth and Opportunity Act (AGOA)

AGOA was signed into law on May 18, 2000 as Title 1 of The Trade and Development Act of 2000 and extended until September 30, 2015.

AGOA's country eligibility requirements are onerous. The Act authorizes the President to designate countries as eligible to receive the benefits of AGOA if they are determined to have established, or are making continual progress toward establishing: market-based economies; the rule of law and political pluralism; elimination of barriers to U.S. trade and investment; protection of intellectual property; efforts to combat corruption; policies to reduce poverty, increasing availability of health care and educational opportunities; protection of human rights and worker rights; and elimination of certain child labor practices. Recognizing the progress Sub-Saharan African countries have been making in these areas, AGOA provides at present preferred access to the U.S. market for 40 of the 48 countries in Sub-Saharan Africa.

---

[7]In addition to the schemes described in the Annex which are focused on Africa and the LDCs, developed countries have also established so called Generalized Schemes of Preferences (GSP) for developing countries more generally, that (except for Canada) are not that relevant for most Sub-Saharan Africa as they involve less advantageous tariff preferences and product coverage.

However, as eligibility is not limited to the relatively poor countries in Sub-Saharan Africa, this group includes the Upper Middle Income Countries (UMIC) in the region,[8] with per capita incomes above $4000, which are much better positioned to make use of such preferences. As a consequence, the countries that really need such access hardly benefit: overall, 90% of exports under AGOA are petroleum products. Of the $3.5 billion in non-oil AGOA exports in 2008, about $2 billion were automobiles, manufactured in South Africa with massive domestic subsidies and limited job creation.[9] Just over $1 billion was clothing, mostly from Kenya, Lesotho, Madagascar, Mauritius, and Swaziland.[10]

AGOA's product coverage is less than generous. It removes tariffs on roughly 98% of products, but excludes key agricultural products, such as cotton, exactly those in which poor African countries have a comparative advantage and the sector that employs the vast majority of the poor. Restrictions on imports of sugar and dairy products effectively discourage African cocoa exporters from processing cocoa beans into chocolate and other value-added products.

As with all preferential schemes there are complex rules of origin which limit the number of products eligible for preferential treatment (see below).

Another problem with AGOA is that the preferences are granted through an unpredictable political process and for a limited time.[11] This uncertainty deters both exporters and investors. The program is scheduled to expire in 2015 and while the Obama administration is committed to renewal, the decision is up to Congress.

European Preferential Schemes

Everything but Arms (EBA). EBA entered into force on March 5, 2001. It allows all imports to the EU from the Least Developed

---

[8]Angola; Botswana; Gabon; Mauritius; Namibia; the Seychelles; and South Africa.

[9]IPS, http://www.ipsnews.net/2013/04/should-south-african-taxpayers-subsidise-car-making-robots/.

[10]Elliot, K., "Reviving AGOA," CDG Brief. Washington: Center for Global Development, 2010.

[11]Presently Zimbabwe and Sudan, Eritrea and Central African Republic are excluded.

Countries duty-free and quota-free (DFQF), i.e. completely free access except for armaments.

Country coverage is limited to the group of Least Developed Countries (LDCs), which encompasses 27 countries in Sub-Saharan Africa. This is problematic, as regional integration is presently high on the political agenda of SSA—as it should be. But these efforts span both LDCs and non-LDCs (e.g. Ghana, Kenya, and Nigeria), complicating the creation of truly common markets in the region.[12] More fundamentally, by limiting this preferential access to LDCs, EBA excludes the countries that are low-income[13] or lower-middle income,[14] which are precisely those African countries best-placed to take advantage of preferences for export diversification.[15] These are the countries which have a minimum range of complementary capabilities that are close to the threshold of developing globally competitive clusters of activity.

The present disaggregation of industrial production processes across several countries has potential for the region.[16] But the economies of poor small countries are simply too narrow. In order to be able to specialize in a limited range of activities (or transformation steps) and participate in such value chains, they must be able to rely on their neighbors to provide necessary inputs Excluding the most feasible locations (Kenya, Ghana) also denies opportunities for their poorer neighbors (Tanzania; Liberia).

Product coverage is very generous (99.8%); currently it only excludes arms and ammunitions, although there were transitional arrangements for bananas, sugar and rice until January 2006, July 2009 and September 2009 respectively. The complexity of its rules of origin has recently led the EU to efforts to improve liberalize them.

---

[12]ECOWAS, the Economic Community of West African States; CEMAC, la Communauté Economic et Monétaire de l'Afrique Central; SADC, the Southern African Development Community; EAC, the East African Development Community and ESA (Eastern and Southern Africa).

[13]Kenya and Zimbabwe.

[14]Cameroon; Cape Verde; Congo; Cote d'Ivoire; Ghana; Lesotho; Nigeria; Sao Tome and Principe; Senegal; South Sudan; Sudan; Swaziland and Zambia.

[15]Greenaway, D.G., P. Collier, and A. Venables, "Rethinking Trade Preferences: How Africa Can Diversify its Exports," *The World Economy*, Chapter 7, "Global Trade Policy." 2009.

[16]Collier, P. and A. Venables, "Rethinking Trade Preferences: How Africa Can Diversify its Exports," *The World Economy* 30(8), pp. 1326-45, 2007.

European Partnerships Agreements (EPAs). For decades the EU has granted preferential access to the EU market for its former colonies in Africa, the Pacific and the Caribbean (the ACP countries). As these preferential arrangements became incompatible with WTO rules, the EU since 2002 has been trying to replace them with "Economic Partnership Agreements" with regional groupings in SSA, the Pacific and the Caribbean, which are reciprocal, and presumably open to all developing countries in the region.

This course of action was unfortunate for several reasons. Given the limited capacity for trade negotiations of most countries in the region, their efforts should have focused on the much more relevant Doha Round and on deeper integration within the African market.

Moreover, the requirement of reciprocity and coverage of substantial all trade in such agreements are not appropriate given the state of development of most of the region; and the EU included issues that go beyond trade in goods (services, intellectual property, government procurement, abolishing export duties, etc.). This will create unnecessarily burdensome obligations for these countries and may distract from or could be inconsistent with their more immediate development priorities.

Also, the membership of the various African groupings overlap; and most of them include members (LDCs) that already have access through the EBA scheme, creating problems for groupings that have common external tariffs.

Thus it is no surprise that, though a few interim agreements were signed, since the launch of EPA negotiations in 2002, with January 1, 2008 as deadline, no EPA has been signed and ratified with any of the African groupings, and many African countries do not see the rationale for continuing such negotiations. In the meantime the EU has upped the stakes in the game by threatening to remove from the current duty free treatment under Regulation 1528/2007 by October 1, 2014 those non least developed countries that have not ratified and implemented their interim EPA.

The time has come for the EU to reconsider its trade policy vis-à-vis Sub-Saharan Africa.

Other Schemes: Canada and Brazil[17]

Canada's Least Developed Countries' Tariff Program (LDCT) entered into force on January 1, 2003, and was extended until June 30, 2014. It is a part of but more generous than Canada's GSP.[18] Just like the EBA it covers only LDCs and is applied to 98.8% of products, excluding dairy, eggs and poultry.

Brazil's preferential scheme covers LDCs only and is to apply to 80% of tariff lines. There is little information covering its details.[19]

A New Approach

From the standpoint of a foreign investor deciding on a project, an African exporter looking for markets or an African government official deciding on a policy, the present hodgepodge system of preferences is a nightmare: different schemes cover different countries, with different product coverage and different rules of origin. No wonder transaction costs in Africa are high. There are many things that African governments can do to help themselves and reduce these costs. But they can do nothing about these.

It makes sense to try to rationalize country, product coverage and rules. The proposed U.S.-EU partnership agreement provides an opportunity for the international community to act and do something that needs to be done any way. It will not be easy, as each scheme reflects the foreign policy interests as well as the domestic protectionist lobbies' pressures on trade policy.

The 2012 Report of a Transatlantic Task Force on Trade and Investment promoting the TTIP acknowledges that "the capacity of such an agreement to generate positive systemic consequences, and improve conditions for trade beyond the Atlantic region, depends on the design of a transatlantic trade agreement and how it links up with common EU and U.S. initiatives with other countries;" the Task Force

---

[17]Norway and Switzerland also have preferential programs, similar to the EU's EBA.

[18]See note 2.

[19]WTO, "Market Access for Products and Services of Export Interest to LDCs," Note by the Secretariat, Sub-Committee on Least-Developed Countries. WT/COMTD/LDC/W/48/Rev.1., March, 2011, pp. 28-29.

also advocates that it should include the integration, harmonization and modernization of their current preferential trade agreements (PTAs) with third countries, to "limit the negative effects of trade diversion and help to reduce so-called "spaghetti-bowl" effects.[20]

On country coverage it is difficult to justify a North America-EU trade arrangement that provides different developing country treatment. What particular European foreign policy interest would be served by the EU and the United States providing different access to Kenya's products? The main problem would be extending DFQF to countries other than the LDCs because of the range of products these countries can export—although if the United States is prepared to accommodate low income countries in AGOA, why can't the EU and Canada or for that matter Brazil do the same?

The changes in product coverage are simple but politically difficult, as they run against protectionist interests everywhere. For example, the United States has only been able to agree to provide DFQF to LDCs on 97% of its product lines which permits to exclude textiles and clothing. But it has been shown that the remaining 3% which is not covered could encompass all of the LDCs main exports.[21]

Finally, there is the question of harmonizing the preferential rules of origin. This is a complex issue which is discussed in detail below. In part rules of origin are used by protectionist interests to limit imports; in part they reflect legitimate concerns to ensure that preferential schemes are not abused. Whatever their motivation, their multiplicity is a serious constraint in the utilization of preferences and creating economies of scale and would have to be addressed in any effort to harmonize preferential arrangements that improve market access for Sub-Saharan countries.

---

[20]"A New Era for Transatlantic Trade Leadership," *Report from the Transatlantic Task Force on Trade and Investment*, co-chaired by Ewa Björling and Jim Kolbe, The European Centre for International Political Economy (ECIPE) and the German Marshall Fund of the United States (GMF), 2012.

[21]Laborde, D., "Looking for a meaningful Duty Free Quota Free Market Access Initiative in the Doha Development Agenda," Issue Paper 4. Geneva: ICTSD, 2008.

Rules of Origin

Simple granting of tariff preference is not enough; they have to be used. But all preference schemes are underutilized, some more than others. Obviously there may be supply constraints. But a common problem is the complexity of requirements exporters need to meet to benefit especially with regard to the preferential rules of origin (RoO).

Rules of origin define how much processing must take place locally before goods and materials are considered to be the product of the exporting country. Goods that comply with the conditions set by the RoO are rewarded with preferential market access, while non-compliant goods are subject to a country's normal treatment of such imports.

Thus, RoO determine whether an exporter will benefit from preferential treatment in the market of the preferential trading partner. Rules of origin may be an important factor in investment decisions if they create uncertainty as to the degree of preferential access that will be available for the finished goods.

The purpose of the preferential rules is to prevent "trade deflection" or simply transshipment, where products from non-beneficiary countries are re-directed through a preference beneficiary, perhaps with minimal working and relabeling to avoid payment of higher customs duties.

Of course, some product-specific RoO go well beyond this objective and are often used as protective devices against the importation of products in which poor countries have some form of competitive advantage: textiles, fish; fish, certain processed agricultural products and a range of light manufactures.

Obviously RoO are needed to ensure preferential regimes actually benefit the economic development of the beneficiary. In order to ensure that the transformation of the product in the processing is "substantial" and not a form of transshipment, typically the rules of origin will require that:

(a) a specific proportion of the total value added—usually around 35% of a product will have taken place in the beneficiary country; and/or

Rules of Origin in the EU EBA Scheme

In the case of the European EBA scheme the RoO defined access so restrictively and inflexibly that the scheme was under-utilized and had minimal impact on LDC exports to the EU. A decade after the introduction of EBA the European Commission acknowledged "a correlation was indeed proven between the stringency of the rules of origin and the utilization rates of the tariff preferences. In addition, product specific rules were considered too complicated. Lastly, compliance was considered too costly and burdensome, both for exporters and administrations."[22] The EU introduced revised rules of origin as of January 1, 2011, simplifying and liberalizing the rules especially for EBA beneficiaries. For example, for most industrial products, the threshold of valued-added required from LDCs was reduced to 30% (against 50% for non-LDCs). For textiles and clothing, single transformation has been granted without quotas. And EBA's cumulation provisions were changed to facilitate limited cumulation between countries of a regional group with different levels of market access to the EU.

To what extent these changes are sufficient to increase utilization remains to be seen.

(b) that the product has undergone sufficient transformation so as to be classified in a different tariff category—e.g. a piece of cloth is turned into a dress.

This sounds simple enough, but in practice it is a daunting obstacle.

First, traders have to adhere to requirements for providing documentation on compliance with the relevant RoO, based on (at times) complicated cost accounting and apportionment, detailed and lengthy record keeping, exporter registration and so forth. Administrative costs are not limited to traders, but also represent a burden to customs

---

[22]Laird, S., "A Review of Trade Preference Schemes for the World's Poorest Countries," Issue Paper 25. Geneva: ICTSD, 2012, p. 35.

authorities with limited institutional capacity. The ad valorem cost of RoO is estimated to be about 4%.[23]

Second, RoO can raise production costs, if, to meet the requirements, (parts of) the product must be produced in a different manner or place, than would otherwise be the case. In a globalized world economy with global value chains, competitiveness must be based on the freedom to source inputs from the most suitable and least expensive location.

Third, these rules can be prohibitive to participate in a global value chain if they require substantial value added in the beneficiary country: many countries in SSA typically do not have enough industrial capacity or the investment climate to attract upstream suppliers of capital intensive inputs and intermediate products needed to produce sufficient domestic value added or to provide competitively prices inputs into a sellable processed product.[24]

In order to deal with this problem, preferential schemes permit *cumulation*. This allows inputs from other countries within a cumulation zone to be counted as being of local origin when further processed there. Bilateral cumulation between the preference-giving and preference-receiving countries also allows inputs sourced from the one party to be considered as originating in the exporting country (and thus counted as local content) when further processed there. For example, under AGOA an African garment manufacturer/exporter imports fabric from the United States, produces garments with the fabric, and exports the garment to the United States. Other forms of cumulation permit countries in a regional group to contribute products for further processing by regional trade partners.

Cumulation thus permits parties to a preferential trade agreement with a region to jointly fulfill the relevant local processing requirements and reduces the restrictiveness of the relevant RoO.

Regional cumulation is particularly relevant, in the case of schemes limited to LDCs, which often belong to the same Customs Unions

---

[23]Francois, J., B. Hoekman, and Manchin, "Preference Erosion and Multilateral Trade Liberalization." *World Bank Economic Review* 20 (2), 2006.

[24]Francois, J. et al., "Opening Markets for the Poorest Countries: Assessing the Effects of Duty-Free, Quota-Free to the G20," mimeo, World Bank, 2011.

Rules of Origin in U.S. AGOA

The general rule of origin for AGOA, with respect to non-apparel products, is that the sum of the cost or value of materials produced in the beneficiary country plus the direct costs of processing must equal at least 35% of the appraised value of the article at the time of its entry into the United States. While the rules permit limited bilateral cumulation (up to 15% out of 35% of "local" materials may comprise U.S. materials) and full cumulation between AGOA beneficiaries, a value-added requirement of 35% is likely to be difficult for many small developing countries.

However, for apparel products AGOA introduced a so-called special rule, allowing African clothing manufacturers flexibility in sourcing fabrics, provided beneficiary countries established effective visa systems and institute required enforcement and verification procedures before any of their apparel exports to the United States can receive AGOA benefits. 26 poorer African countries exporting apparel to the United States were allowed to use fabric from any origin (single transformation) and still meet the criteria for preferential access. This simplification contributed to an increase in export volume of about 168% for the top seven beneficiaries or approximately four times as much as the 44% growth effect from the initial preference access under the Africa Growth Opportunity Act without the single transformation proving that a bold approach to rules of origin can provoke substantial supply responses from developing countries and help them build a more diversified export base.[25]

(e.g. the East African Community (EAC) and the Southern African Customs Union (SACU), with non-LDC neighbors, which thus need to be included in expanded cumulation.

To allow cumulation it is helpful in addressing the problem of limited value added in processing, but adds another layer of complexity in

---

[25]World Bank, Doing Business Project-Trading Across Borders http://www.doingbusiness.org/data/exploretopics/trading-across-borders.

Rules of Origin and Canada's Least-Developed Country Tariff (LDCT)

To qualify for the LDCT up to 75% of a final product's value may originate outside the beneficiary country. However, Canada offers attractive cumulation possibilities to LDC beneficiaries by permitting global cumulation with all other beneficiaries of the Canadian GSP scheme. This means that of the 40% local content requirement a portion could have been sourced from other GSP beneficiaries. Bilateral cumulation is also permitted with Canada as the preference giving country.

---

the documentation needed to ensure that a particular product is eligible for preferences as the origin of all the inputs needs to be traced and documented.

A fourth problem with RoO is that preference granting countries employ substantially *different methodologies* to define origin and oblige beneficiary producers to adapt their manufacturing processes in order to comply with the various conditions that they impose.

As a result, developing countries are faced with a myriad of rules, depending on the export destination. These are often incompatible with each other or substantially different and undermine potential economies of scale. For example, an exporter based in Tanzania will face different rules when exporting goods to Europe, the United States, or Canada, each of which also differs when compared to the RoO under the regional COMESA trade agreement. The differences in these rules impedes diversification in Sub-Saharan Africa, as it is easier to diversify by selling products that have been successfully been sold in one market into other markets than selling different products into more markets[26] as new investments may need to be made to penetrate each new market. This imposes a substantial administrative burden: the associated costs are often too high for exporters in many poor countries[27] and undermine achieving economies of scale.

---

[26]Francois et al., *op. cit.*, p. 10.

[27]This helps explain why Lesotho has significant exports of apparel to the United States, but not to the EU.

The fifth and most fundamental problem with current RoO is that, since their creation decades ago, the world globalized: production of a good became fragmented between many countries, with each specializing in one narrow task. Comparative advantages are less and less at the level of whole products, but simply a specific transformation step. So RoO based on the assumption that a poor country can create a significant share of value added are unrealistic and a strong limitation in promoting manufacturing specialization. The reality is that in Sub-Saharan Africa few inputs are available domestically often because of the capital-intensive character of the production for example cloth: the economies are narrow and need to rely on their neighbors to provide necessary inputs in order to take advantage of the preferences rather than import from the most competitive sources.

In the meantime, today's global value chains hold potential for Africa since it is much easier to develop capabilities in a narrow range of tasks than in integrated, vertical production of an entire product.[28] But for trade preferences to able to act as a catalyst for manufacturing exports, they need to be designed to be consistent with international trade in fragmented tasks (as opposed to complete products) and need to be open to countries with sufficient levels of complementary inputs such as skills and infrastructure.

As labor-intensive export manufacturing is the key to African job creation and growth, it is time to update trade preferences to be relevant to the current disaggregation of production processes across countries.

For RoO to allow countries to specialize in a narrow range of activities, or "tasks" they should not set too high a threshold for local content: if the value-added requirement is low enough, there is no need for cumulation: a low value-added requirement common across all products would be more transparent, simpler for firms to satisfy, and easier to administer by customs and other agencies. Substantial cumulation should be permitted of inputs sourced from other countries. There is little reason cumulation should not be possible on a much wider scale, for example in all goods and materials that are already duty-free in the EU and the United States or within the FTAs with

---

[28]Collier, P., www.agoa.info/news.php?story=1274, 2012.

other bilateral trade partners. Expanding the cumulation provisions for Sub-Saharan Africa could help unlock trade flows and improve the region's market access.

AGOA has an innovative feature, which has contributed to a very substantial expansion of some developing country exports: the United States has established an inspection program in these countries to verify/certify that sufficient processing has occurred. This "extra-territorial enforcement" in the sense that importing countries invest in establishing certification systems in developing countries to determine that exporters do not engage in simple transshipment and satisfy the origin rules before consignments are shipped, has been helpful in reducing transaction costs and facilitating utilization of preferences.[29] Similarly, for agricultural and fish products both the EU and the United States require local veterinary and sanitary inspection of slaughter houses and fish processing facilities by their own inspection teams in country as a condition for unbothered market entry. But as the exporter is often expected to pay for this, it increases costs. And the presence of foreign inspectors in country may not be an agreeable solution to some many developing countries.

How to Move Forward

The key to reform is to adopt the best elements of each scheme that were effective in helping utilization of preference and attempt to harmonize them across preferences granting countries.

Product coverage is key to permitting a balanced development: preferences should include products that developing countries can produce competitively. In this respect the EU's EBA with its 100% coverage is far superior to the U.S. scheme. The exclusion of key agricultural products is a serious gap in the U.S. program: for sugar, tobacco, and peanut exporters, tight restrictions on access to the U.S. market constitute a serious barrier.

While agriculture provides livelihoods for roughly two-thirds of all Africans, total exports of food, beverages, and tobacco products from AGOA-eligible countries grew just 5% annually from 2001 to 2009.

---

[29]Francois et al, *op. cit.*

Including these products would allow, for example, Malawi, Mozambique, and Zambia to gain access for their currently excluded sugar, peanut, and tobacco exports.[30]

Regarding country coverage, the United States is far more generous, as the EBA scheme is limited to LDCs. However, AGOA seems too generous: with no income per capita restrictions, the bulk of the benefits may go, as they do in AGOA, to countries like South Africa that do not need it. Thus, the program should be limited to countries with per capita income less than $4000, excluding higher middle income countries as classified by the World Bank Atlas.

Regarding rules of origin, liberal rules that allow for a significant use of imported inputs and permit cumulation of inputs sourced in other developing countries have played a major role in the cases where exports of manufactures have grown significantly.[31] Best practices include a low domestic value-added threshold (e.g. 25% as applied by Canada); and permitting cumulation allowing for inputs to be used from any developing country that is granted preferences (Canada; AGOA special origin regime), as this allow producers in LDCs to source inputs from the lowest cost suppliers, of course provided that their own tariffs for these inputs do not undermine this.

The one clear advantage of the AGOA program is its rule of origin for clothing exports (with the caveat regarding the presence of "extraterritorial' inspectors).Thus Collier advocates for a "Global" AGOA: an expansion of the current trade preference program to allow all African exports, not just LDC's, preferential access to all OECD markets. "The trade preferences offered by AGOA is like the "pump priming mechanisms" that are helping African nations to break into manufacturing and the global market."[32]

---

[30]Elliot, K., "Open Markets for the Poorest Countries: Trade Preferences That Work," CGD Working Group on Global Trade Preference Reform. Washington: Center for Global Development, 2010.

[31]Francois et. al, *op. cit.*, p. 26.

[32]Collier, *op. cit.*

Conclusion and Recommendations

The timing is right for a new initiative to help Sub-Saharan Africa benefit from trading opportunities in today's increasingly globalized world. Such effort would harmonize country and product coverage; and rules of origin of the different preferential arrangements currently in place, taking the best features and most effective provisions of their respective programs, making them compatible and updating the rules to the current trading environment.

This initiative would fit well with the new U.S.-EU Transatlantic Trade and Investment Partnership, which would benefit from harmonization of agreements with third countries anyway. But instead of being just one of many issues on the EU-U.S. negotiations agenda somewhere in the future, focusing on the urgent needs of Sub-Saharan Africa now, as a precursor to the overall agreement, would help the region's economic transformation, give a tremendous push to its integration in the world economy, and lift millions of people out of poverty.

Such an action would be in keeping with the spirit of the Marshall Plan when the United States allowed Europe to give priority to regional cooperation and integration, while allowing asymmetric full market access for European exporters to the U.S. market in the meantime.

In order to make solidarity with Sub-Saharan Africa a truly transatlantic endeavor, obviously Canada, which has often showed political willingness to help poor countries through trade arrangements, should join. But to amplify the benefits of the initiative, Latin American countries should also be invited to join as preference-givers, building upon their intentions expressed in the WTO to improve market access for poorer developing countries.

Recommendations

Country coverage. In order for the initiative to benefit those countries that need it most, without excluding only slightly less poor countries that can make use of the preferences, the initiative should focus on all low income and lower middle-income countries in Sub-Saharan Africa, i.e., countries with per capita income less than $4,035. Thus, the United States should exclude the higher middle-income countries (notably South Africa) that presently qualify for AGOA, while the EU and Canada should expand their schemes, presently focused on LDCs only, to include all Lower and Lower Middle Income Countries in Sub-Saharan Africa.

Product coverage should be 100% DFQF. Most SSA countries' exports are highly specialized, producing a very narrow scope of goods; in many cases, a few raw materials account for most of their exports.[33] Excluding even a small number of product exclusions can rob the initiative of any meaning as in most developed country markets, 3% of tariff lines cover between 90% and 98% of exports from LDCs.[34]

The U.S. AGOA and the Canadian preferences program for LDCs presently do not cover all products: they should be expanded to include particularly those in which these countries have a comparative advantage: agriculture and labor-intensive manufacturing products, including apparel and footwear.

Ensure that the Preferential Rules of Origin provide genuine market access. For Sub-Saharan Africa to be able to exploit preferential access, qualification requirements have to be relevant, simple and harmonized across preference givers. Updating the preferential RoO to the realities of production networks that define trading conditions in the 21st century is long overdue, as is international agreement on the methodology to define origin in order to harmonize these rules.

Negotiations on RoO have been dragging on for many years at the WTO without any results. While regulatory alignment is an essential part of the trade agreement as envisaged between the EU and the United States, even these negotiations will be complex and thus time consuming.

---

[33]Oil and gas (Angola, Chad, Equatorial Guinea, Sudan); iron ore (Mauritania); diamonds (Central Africa Republic, Liberia, Sierra Leone); copper (Zambia); aluminum (Mozambique); agricultural crops like cocoa (Sao Tome, Togo), cotton (Benin, Burkina Faso, Mali, Togo).

[34]Bouet, A. et al., "The Costs and Benefits of Duty-Free, Quota-Free Market Access for Poor Countries: Who and What Matters." CGD Working Paper. Washington: Center for Global Development, 2010; Laborde, *op. cit.*

In the meantime, the unilateral rules that guide exports from Sub-Saharan Africa could be relaxed to ensure genuine utilization of preferential market access.

A low value-added requirement (10 or 15%) common across all products would be transparent, simple for firms to satisfy, and easy to administer.[35] If the value-added requirement is low enough, there is no need for cumulation. But then there is little stimulus to increased industrialization and local processing. Thus a somewhat higher value-added threshold may be more desirable, in which case generous cumulation should be allowed, preferably regional, i.e. all of Sub-Saharan Africa.

To deal with the differences of how RoO are defined, firms could be allowed to choose among different equivalent rules—for example, either a percentage[36] of locally added value, or simple transformation (change in tariff heading).

The simplest way to create the necessary flexibility, which does not need any negotiations among the TTIP partners,[37] would be mutual recognition of origin regimes across preference givers, accepting an import eligible in one market as eligible in any other; and allowing extended cumulation, so beneficiaries can cumulate inputs from all developing countries and FTA partners.

Ensure better transparency and predictability, and therefore, promote trade and investment, by making preferences permanent or long lasting. As continuation of giving preferences is up to the benevolence of the preference granting country lack of stability and predictability of such programs discourages investment in potential export sectors. The uncertainty that is associated with preference regimes that are changed frequently and may expire if not renewed periodically by parliaments (e.g. AGOA) can have very negative effects on investment decisions.[38]

---

[35]Brenton, P., "Enhancing Trade Preferences for LDCs: Reducing the Restrictiveness of Rules of Origin" in Richard Newfarmer (ed.), *Trade, Doha and Development: a Window into the Issues*. Washington, DC: World Bank, 2005.

[36]The Blair Commission proposed a value-added requirement on all products of no more than 10%.

[37]Elliot, K., 2010, *op. cit.*

[38]Phelps N., J. Stillwell and R. Wanjiru, "Broken chain? Foreign direct investment in the Kenyan clothing industry," *World Development* 37(2), pp. 314-325, 2008.

Ideally, in order to provide certainty to investors regarding the applicable policy regime over a long time horizon, preferences should be granted on a permanent basis preferably by binding them in the WTO.[39] If periodic reviews are unavoidable, sufficiently long lasting (a minimum of 10 years) to provide the security to investors for real market access to materialize.

Latin American countries join the new market access initiative. Even with the limitations spelled out above regarding access to the U.S., European and Canadian markets, with the exception of agriculture the main problems exporters in Sub-Saharan Africa face in international markets are protection in other developing countries, where barriers to trade are generally higher than in OECD countries. Some countries in Sub-Saharan Africa (particularly low income countries in east and south/central Africa) would benefit more from concessions from non-OECD G20 countries.[40] Moreover, in most of the cases the technical and phyto-sanitary requirements of developing countries are much easier for African exporters to meet than the comparable non-tariff barriers in OECD markets.

The potential for a more rapid growth in African exports to these countries is significantly understated, as emerging markets are growing at twice the rate of OECD countries, from which demand may remain depressed. Preferential access to these dynamic markets could have an enormous impact on SSA exports, as South-South trade gathers greater momentum.

---

[39]Francois et. al., *op cit.*, p. 30.
[40]Ibid., p 12.

ANNEX

Measures in favor of exports originating from LDCs or SSA

Preference granting country	Description	Beneficiaries	Coverage/margin of preference
Brazil	Duty-free and Quota-free scheme for LDCs	LDCs	Duty-free and Quota-free access for products from LDCs covering 80% of all tariff lines to be granted by mid-2010.
Canada	GSP – Least-developed Countries' Tariff Programme (LDCT) Entry into force: January 1, 2003, extended until June 30, 2014	LDCs	With the exception of over-quota tariff items for dairy, poultry and egg products, Canada provides duty-free access under all tariff items for imports from LDCs
EU	GSP - Everything But Arms (EBA) initiative Entry into force: March 5, 2001	LDCs	Since October 1, 2009, the EBA has been granting DFQF access for all products from all LDCs (except arms and ammunitions). The EU introduced revised rules of origin for the GSP, as of January 1, 2011, simplifying rules specially for the LDCs,
	Economic Partnership Agreements (EPAs)	79 African, Caribbean and Pacific (ACP) countries, 40 of which are LDCs	EPAs include provision for duty-free and quota-free market access. Interim EPAs are signed by the following LDCs: (i) Southern African Development Community (SADC): Lesotho and Mozambique; (ii) Eastern and Southern Africa (ESA): Madagascar (signatures by Comoros and Zambia are pending). Interim EPAs are initialed with the East African Community (EAC), which includes four LDCs: Burundi, Rwanda, Tanzania and Uganda.
United States	GSP for least-developed beneficiary developing countries (LDBDC) Entry into force: January 1, 1976, (further extensions are currently being considered)	43 designated LDCs	In addition to the standard GSP coverage of nearly 5,000 products, 1,450 articles exclusively available for LDC beneficiaries for duty-free treatment
	African Growth and Opportunity Act (AGOA) Entry into force: May 2000, extended until September 30, 2015	38 designated Sub-Saharan African Countries (including 25 LDCs)	1,835 products, including textiles and apparel, available for duty-free treatment, in addition to duty-free treatment on products benefitting from GSP.

Chapter 4

Reshaping the South Atlantic: Can the BICs Bring it About?

Jorge Heine and Deborah Farias

"The Atlantic is no more than a river between Africa and South America"
President Luiz Inacio Lula da Silva, 2006.

For much of the second half of the past century, the world was largely steered from the North Atlantic. The Anglo-American "special relationship," or *entente*, was the axis on which this rested until 1975 or so. It was gradually replaced by the G7 from that year onwards. The addition of France, Germany, Italy and Japan, plus Canada, meant that this exclusive partnership was no longer monopolized by English-speaking peoples (as Churchill would have put it), but over time the G7 developed into a critical, if informal, forum to address complex issues of macro-economic coordination among the world's most advanced economies. The G7, conceived by two brilliant finance ministers turned government leaders, Valery Giscard d'Estaing and Helmut Schmidt, served the world well for some twenty years.

Yet the so-called "Asian crisis" of 1997, originating in Thailand, but soon to envelop much of East and Southeast Asia, with reverberations throughout the world economy, brought the G7 into question. The group was confronted with a crisis "east of Suez" about whose dynamics its members knew little, and had little legitimacy to act upon. Moreover, many considered that the advice proffered by the Western-led international financial institutions s on how to solve the problem made it only worse, deepening the downward economic spiral in which several Asian countries found themselves.

One response to this challenge was the creation of the G20 at finance minister level in December 1999, a group led by the Canadian Finance Minister Paul Martin. By bringing in many of the larger emerging economies into the "inner circle" of global economic coordination, at least a measure of first-hand knowledge about what was happening was deployed beyond the rarefied atmosphere of the North Atlantic. This would turn out to be only the opening shot in a major realignment in the making. Referred to as "the acronym that defined the decade without a name," BRICs, the term coined by Goldman Sachs in 2001 to encompass Brazil, Russia, India and China, soon became the coin of the realm. These four countries, known for their large land mass, large populations and growing economies, were projected to overtake the combined product of the six most industrialized economies by 2050, thus altering the conventional view of the extant international order. The 2008-2009 financial crisis, triggered in the United States and with devastating consequences for the eurozone, but which only marginally affected the BRIC countries, only ratified this notion. The liberal international order that emerged after the end of the Cold War under the hegemonic leadership of the United States found itself under increasing strains. Yet, the precise contours of the new order remain undefined.

It is a time of transition in world politics, and much will depend on some key choices to be made in years to come to set the course for the newly emerging international system. For some, there is little doubt this will be the "Asian century," by which they mean the century of China and of India. For others, it will be the Pacific century, something seemingly ratified by the growing prominence of the once obscure Asia-Pacific Economic Cooperation (APEC) forum. Robert D. Kaplan takes this one step further, arguing that it is the Indian Ocean where the future lies, and that Calcutta will be the next global city.[1]

Yet despite all the difficulties of the North Atlantic economies (though Canada remains in enviably good shape), the Atlantic area is still very much at the center of worldwide trade and investment flows. Perhaps what is needed is a radical rethinking of the relative weight of the until-now dominant North and the more low-profile South Atlantic.

---

[1]Robert D. Kaplan, *Monsoon: The Indian Ocean and the Future of American Power*. New York: Random House, 2010.

The South Atlantic Means South America and Sub-Saharan Africa

Latin America and Africa (plus Asia), were until not too long ago part of what used to be known as the Third World, a term now replaced by "Global South." East, South- and Southeast Asia are now the fastest-growing areas in the world—in fact, six of 10 fastest growing economies are in Africa—and are at the very core of the forces reshaping the new global order. Sub-Saharan Africa and South America, on the other hand, have traditionally been seen as marginal subcontinents, far removed from the Eurasian geopolitical center. They share a history of economic underdevelopment, of political instability, of legendary dictators, of social and economic inequality, and of inward-orientation. African countries achieved their independence more recently, and their state formation and institutional development is correspondingly weaker.[2]

There are more countries in Africa (54) than in Latin America (33), though the per capita income of the latter is considerably higher. Given that, by definition, an exercise such as rethinking what the Atlantic Basin is all about is geopolitical rather than cultural, it would also be useful to circumscribe the limits of the geographic area we are looking at. Conceptually, then, the ideal is to focus not so much on Africa as a whole or on the totality of Latin America and the Caribbean (LAC) but on specific sub-regions within each of these continents—i.e., Sub-Saharan Africa and South America. The reasons for this are not difficult to justify. The Maghreb, i.e., Northern Africa, looks largely to the Mediterranean, and responds to a very different social and economic matrix than the rest of Africa. The case of South America is somewhat different, since its societies have a lot more in common with those of Central America and Mexico, than, say, Nigeria does with Egypt. That said, over the past decade or so, there has been a growing divergence between the South American region and its neighbors to the North. Both parts of the Latin-American/Caribbean (LAC) region have been pulled increasingly apart.

---

[2]There are exceptions. The South African state has greater capacity than that of a number of Latin American countries.

Mexico, and the Central American and Caribbean nations, by and large not endowed with enormous amounts of natural resources, have come to depend more and more on *maquiladoras* producing for the U.S. market, on tourism and on the drug trade. On all fronts, from migration flows to sports to cultural exchanges to organized crime, they are becoming more and more integrated into the U.S. (and, to a lesser extent, the Canadian) mode of production. Chinese competition on the manufacturing front (from electronics to textiles) has been especially deleterious to industry in these parts of the Americas. As a rule, economic growth here has been lower and social problems more serious. El Salvador, Guatemala and El Salvador have the highest murder rates in the world.

South America, on the other hand, has gone in a very different direction. Richly endowed with natural resources, from abundant agricultural land to plentiful fresh water and ample mineral reserves, both oil and non-oil, it has made the most of the commodities boom of the past decade. It is South American countries like Argentina, Brazil, Chile and Peru that have made the most of the growing demand from the Asian giants, though other countries have not done too badly either. In 2009, at the height of the financial crisis, the country with the highest growth in the Americas was Bolivia, with 3.4%, and in 2010, Paraguay grew at an astounding 14.5%, a rate comparable to that of the Gulf States or Singapore. Trade and investment flows here point increasingly toward Asia. For Brazil and Chile, China is their # 1 trading partner (combined exports and imports), having long displaced the United States. Argentina and Peru should follow suit shortly. Venezuela is doing its best to diversify its oil exports, targeting Asian markets in general and China in particular. Migration flows from South American countries to the U.S. are minimal, and U.S. influence is ebbing.

Beyond the economic forces at play, a number of key political developments have given special impetus to the rise of South America as a stand-alone entity, with its own dynamics and personality, something it arguably never really had in a past riven by rivalries and differences. Mexico's joining of NAFTA in 1994 meant that the one Latin American country that could have balanced Brazil within the broader Latin American region, essentially "opted out" of the Latin American project. The War on Terror unleashed by Washington after 9/11 led to the United States becoming engaged elsewhere, paying little attention to what happened in the Western Hemisphere. And the unraveling of the Free Trade Area of the Americas (FTAA) project, scheduled to be in place by 2005, but that fell apart much earlier, put paid to the most ambitious undertaking to spread "deep globalization" in this part of the world.

The formal emergence of the *Unión de Naciones Sudamericanas* (UNASUR) in 2008, first led by Chilean president Michelle Bachelet, was in many ways the culmination of South America's rise as an international entity. It was quickly followed by the launch of the South American Defense Council, a signal that even the "hard" areas of international politics would not be exempt from this trend towards a more assertive regionalism, one fed by the collective diplomacy that has become such a hallmark of Latin American foreign policies in the post-Cold War era.

In the course of the past two decades, democracy has become the norm in South America. The past ten years, in turn, have seen a veritable economic boom, with countries paying down their foreign debt, expanding their hard currency reserves and otherwise being prepared to face external crises, as became manifest in 2008-2009. As Roberto Porzecanski has put it, for the first time in 200 years, a financial crisis in the North did not wreak havoc in the South.

From a very different starting point, Africa has also come a long way. Though by no means fully democratized, free and fair elections and democratic institutions are making headway in the continent, as is economic and social progress. Between 2000 and 2010 six of the ten fastest-growing economies world-wide were African (namely Angola, Nigeria, Ethiopia, Mozambique, Chad and Rwanda).[3] The growing demand for commodities from Asia is one the drivers of this boom, as it has been in South America. Another is the search for markets. With the North Atlantic economies seen as largely mature markets (in some cases, contracting ones), international business is looking for new opportunities. South America and Africa offer those aplenty, at least for those with sufficient stomach to take on what is known as the "Africa risk."

---

[3]Greg Mills and Geoffrey Herbst, *Africa's Third Liberation: The New Search for Prosperity and Jobs.* Johannesburg: Penguin Books, 2012, p. 3.

From marginal, low-growth, politically unstable regions, Africa and South America are thus morphing into something else: the world economy's new frontiers, with high growth rates, responsible economic management and more solid and predictable institutions. What has not changed, however, is that there is very little interaction between them. Despite these recent commonalities and some of their shared historical predicaments, Africans and Latin Americans largely ignore each other. Trade is minimal, as are FDI flows. To some extent, it could be argued that this is inevitable and springs directly from the fact that these are economies that compete, rather than complement each other. On the other hand, it means that many business opportunities go begging.

Chile's case is revealing. Though widely considered to have made the most of globalization with a largely trade-driven foreign policy targeted towards opening foreign markets, Chile has a mere two embassies in the 49 countries of Sub-Saharan Africa, and does very little trade with Africa, apart from buying oil from Nigeria. A significant food exporter (the largest exporter of fresh fruit in the Southern Hemisphere), professedly aiming to become one of the top ten food exporters in the world by 2020, there is much business that Chile could do in Africa, most prominently in the oil exporting nations and in the Portuguese-speaking ones. But it is not taking place.

The only attempt so far to develop a South Atlantic sphere of influence of sorts is not a very encouraging one. It harks back to the days of apartheid-era South Africa and its attempts to create a South Atlantic Treaty Organization (SATO), in a joint venture with the military regimes of the Southern Cone, attempts which never took off.

Brazil as the South Atlantic Hub

Still, there is one country that in the course of the past decade has made an attempt to bridge the South Atlantic, and that is Brazil. As one of the original members of the BRICS, Brazil is at the forefront of the world's emerging powers. And although Brazil has had traditionally an assertive and imaginative foreign policy, its "diplomatic offensive" achieved new heights under President Luiz Inacio Lula da Silva's (2003-2010). At a time when many governments have been closing missions and cutting back on foreign affairs budgets, Brazil, grasping that diplomacy has become more, not less, significant in the age of globalization, did the opposite. During Lula's presidency, Brazil opened some 35 new embassies all around the world, of which it has 136 by now.

In Latin America, Brazil has played a key role. It has been the driving force behind UNASUR, has taken the lead in stabilizing Haiti through MINUSTAH, the first UN peace-keeping mission formed by a majority of Latin American troops and headed by a Brazilian general, and continues to be the leading member of MERCOSUR, the Common Market of the South that has just been joined by Venezuela. Brazil is willing to work with Washington, but not if that entails sacrificing principles such as democratic rule, as shown in the Honduran crisis in 2009-2010.

But perhaps the most remarkable feature of Brazilian diplomacy during the past decade has been its willingness to put Africa ("global capitalism's last frontier")[4] front and center. In his eight years in office, President Lula undertook twelve visits to Africa to 21 countries. His foreign minister, Celso Amorim, made 67 such visits, to 34 African countries. Of the total number of embassies opened by Brazil in these years, more than half—twenty—were opened in Africa, ratcheting up the total to 37, more than the United Kingdom has. African countries, on the other hand, fully grasped the significance of Brazil's new role. Some 17 African embassies were opened in Brasilia in this period, making for the largest number of African missions in any capital in the Southern Hemisphere. Some 47 African kings, presidents and prime ministers visited Brazil in these years.[5]

What makes this Brazilian "charm offensive" in Africa noteworthy is not just these numbers, and Brasilia's willingness to put its money where its mouth is, but also how far its strays from the regional norm.

---

[4]To use the expression of Jose Flavio Sombra Saraiva in his incisive chapter, "A Africa e a politica externa na era Lula: Relancamento da politica atlantica brasileira," in Adriano de Freixo, Luiz Pedone, Thiago Moreira Rodrigues e Vagner Camilo Alves (eds.), *A politica externa brasileira na era Lula: Un balance*. Rio de Janeiro: Apicuri, 2011, p.180.

[5]For these figures see the excellent report *Bridging the Atlantic: Brazil and Africa*. Washington: The World Bank, 2012.

Despite the relative geographical contiguity, for most Latin American countries Africa might as well not exist.

Of the BRICS countries, it is the two "Asian giants," i.e., China and India, which stand out for their high growth rates and their worldwide trade and investment dynamism over the past decade. We shall examine below the growing presence of China and India in Africa (and in LAC). And although there are similarities in the activities of the three BICs countries in that continent, Brazil's motivation and driving force for assigning to Africa a priority few others do, seem somewhat different

The links between Brazil and Africa have long-standing historical roots, going back to the days of slavery and the slave trade. From the 16th to the 19th century, it is estimated that some 3.5 million Africans were transported to Brazil, largely to work in the sugar plantations in Bahia. Although estimates vary, according to the latest census, half the population of Brazil (some 190 million) is made up of Afro-descendants. This makes Brazil the country with the second largest black population in the world after Nigeria. Beyond demography and ethnicity, there are also historical and political links. The ties between Portugal's African colonies (particularly Angola) and Brazil are also of long standing. Angolan representatives took part in Brazil's struggle for independence. At one point the possibility was mooted of Angola joining as another province of an independent Brazil. Fascinatingly, the strongest opposition to such an initiative came not from Portugal but from Britain. Her Majesty's Government required that this be explicitly ruled out, as a condition for recognizing an independent Brazil. One can only speculate as to what such a trans-Atlantic Brazil might have meant for the South Atlantic.

By putting Africa front and center in its foreign policy initiatives, Brazil is not simply adding one more region to Itamaraty's already crowded diplomatic calendar.[6] It is also making a statement. By singling out the least developed continent as an arena for such a display of diplomatic and public policy initiatives, it is saying that in the new

---

[6]On Brazilain foreign policy, see Tullo Vigevani and Gabriel Cepaluni, *Brazilian Foreign Policy in Changing Times: The Quest for Autonomy from Sarney to Lula*. New York: Lexington Books, 2009; Sean W. Burges, *Brazilian Foreign Policy after the Cold War*. Gainesville: University Press of Florida, 2009; and Riordan Roett, *The New Brazil*. Washington DC: Brookings, 2010.

century diplomacy is not just about geopolitics and trade, but also about solidarity and cooperation with those who need it the most.

This is also reflected in the type of cooperation that Brazil is providing to African countries. As a rule, Brazil does not provide cash grants. Rather, it works with African countries in enhancing capacity in areas like agriculture, health and education. Is also refuses to impose the type of conditionality dictated by Western donors, which raises so many objections in Africa. Far from simply attempting to "buy its way into Africa," Brazil has developed and designed a *sui generis* approach to work with Africa "as a trustworthy partner, and not just another donor." Whether this will succeed or not is another matter, but this is the rationale behind it.

The Brazilian approach to this partnership with Africa embodies what the new South-South diplomacy is all about. Brazil is a big country with a well-financed Foreign Ministry, yet it does not have the sort of resources to deploy abroad that the United States or even China has. What Brazil does have is a number of commonalities with Africa in terms of its development challenges, from similar soils, to dealing with pandemics such as AIDS.[7] By enhancing local capacity, training African workers and technicians, and drawing on Brazilian public policy experiences, Brazil positions itself not just as another foreign power trying to extract oil, gold and copper from the African continent, but as something else. Again, this is part and parcel of Brazil's effort to rely on its "diplomatic GDP" to disprove those who say that "there are only two BRICs in the wall," by which they mean China and India, due to their sheer population size.

China and India in South America and Sub-Saharan Africa

Much as Brazil is the "hub" of the South Atlantic, two of the key "spokes" that have made their presence felt in this part of the world over the past decade are China and India. In fact, it could well be argued that a key driver of the economic boom that we have witnessed both in Africa and in Latin America in this period has been the

---

[7] For more on Brazil's foreign policy related to South-South cooperation, see P. Dauvergne and Deborah BL Farias, "The Rise of Brazil as a Global Development Power," *Third World Quarterly*, Volume 33, Issue 5, 2012, pp. 903-917.

demand for commodities arising from the two Asian giants. In the following sections, we undertake a preliminary, comparative analysis of what increased trade with China and India has meant for particularly South America and Sub-Saharan Africa, and how this exponential growth has altered the two sub-continents' relations with the world economy and the international system more generally.[8]

For South America, traditionally dependent on trade with the United States, and for Sub-Saharan Africa, historically focused on Europe, this has entailed a major shift in how they interact with and view the rest of the world.[9] On the face of it, such a growing demand for raw materials and commodities from these two areas can only be beneficial. Who can be against more trade, higher prices for the natural resources of these still developing countries, and the consequent increase in exports and hard currency inflows that all of this entails? Yet, there is a downside to this, to which we shall get to in a moment. But for now, let us examine *seriatim* what has happened with China and India in these two sub-continents.

China and India's Trade with South America

China and India's trade with South America (S.Am.) has increased dramatically from 2000 to 2010. China and India's exports to the region went from $ 4.14 billion (2000) to almost $ 60 billion (2010), while imports grew at a much greater pace, rising from $ 5.47 billion in 2000 to close to $ 92 billion in 2010.

Yet, the region still represents relatively little for both China and India. As Graphs 2A and 2B indicate, in 2010 South America was the destination for 3.87% of total Chinese exports and for 2.66% of Indian exports; in turn, the region was the source of 5.73% of China's and 3.43% of India's total imports. The most visible difference between China and India's trade relations with South America con-

---

[8]The literature on Sino-LAC relations is extensive. See, among other sources, R. Evan Ellis, *China in Latin America: The Whats & Wherefores*. Boulder, Colorado: Lynne Rienner, 2009; Kevin P. Gallagher and Roberto Porzecanski, *The Dragon in the Room: China and the Future of Latin American Industrialization*. Stanford: Stanford University Press, 2010; and Ralf J. Leiteritz, "China y América Latina: el matrimonio perfecto?", *Colombia Internacional* 75 (enero a junio de 2012), pp. 49-81.

[9]See Andrew F. Cooper and Jorge Heine (eds.), *Which Way Latin America? Hemispheric Politics Meets Globalization*. Tokyo: United Nations University Press, 2009.

Graph 1. China and India: Trade with South America

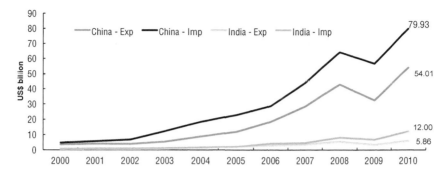

Graph 2A. South America as Destination of China and India's Exports

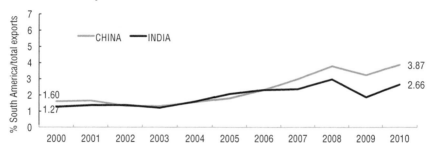

Graph 2B. South America as Origin of China and India's Imports

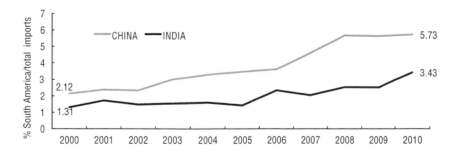

Graph 3A. China and India: Brazil in Total Exports to South America

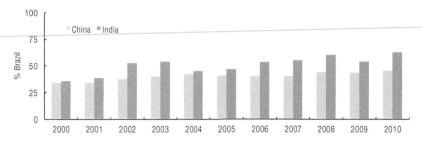

Graph 3B. China and India: Brazil in Total Imports from South America

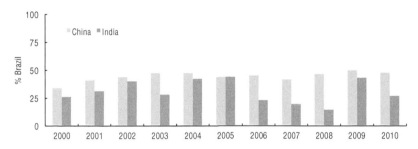

cerns the *volume* of trade. In 2010 India's exports to the area reached $5.84 billion—the equivalent of only 10.8% of China's exports to the region for the same year.

Brazil has consistently and significantly been the biggest buyer of Chinese and Indian products in South America. In 2000 Brazil purchased 34% of combined Chinese and Indian exports to the region, and by 2010 this number had reached almost 50%. Following the same tendency of concentration, the South American giant went from being the origin of 33% (2000) to 45% (2010) of all South American exports to these two Asian countries (see Graphs 3A and 3B).

The increased interaction of China and India with South American countries cannot be understated. Beginning with Brazil—which represents about half of South American GDP—the impact of this increased trade is significant. While the United States was historically the main source of Brazilian imports, its significance has declined

Graph 4. China and India: Exports to South America, Selected Countries

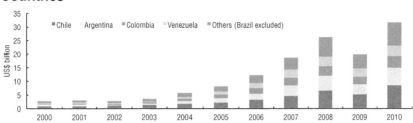

from almost 25% in 2000 to barely over 15% in 2010.[10] In turn, China went from 2.2% to 14.15%, securing a very close second place. More dramatically, while in 2000 U.S.exports to Brazil were 11 times that of China's, in 2010 they were less than 1% higher.

China has risen to the top positions of almost all South American countries' major supplier list. In 2010 it displaced the U.S. to become #1 in Chile. It also surpassed the U.S. in Argentina, where it became #2 (second only to Brazil). China also ranked #2 as a source of imports for Peru (closely behind the U.S.); Venezuela; and Colombia, to name a few.

As for India, it also has improved its position as a supplier to South American countries, although it does not even come close to China's numbers. The most significant case seems to be between India and Brazil as it went from less than half of a percent of Brazil's imports in 2000 to 2.3% in 2010. Although relatively low, India still managed to get into Brazil's top 10 list of suppliers in 2010.

Shifting to China and India as buyers of South American goods, the first point to be made is that India's numbers have oscillated substantially. During 2000-2010, the top spot of South American exporter to India was occupied four times by Brazil, three times by Argentina, twice by Chile and twice by Venezuela. Brazil has shown the most consistent growth in exports to India: from $ 0.18 billion (2000) to $ 3.22 billion (2010). Venezuela has been also come to the fore: in 2008

---

[10]Note: the data here is based on what was reported by each importing country (ex: Brazil's imports from China); because of exchange rate variation there are discrepancies with the exact numbers from exporting countries (ex: China's exports to Brazil). However, this is not expected to change the end result significantly.

Graph 5A. Brazil's Exports to U.S., China, India, and Argentina

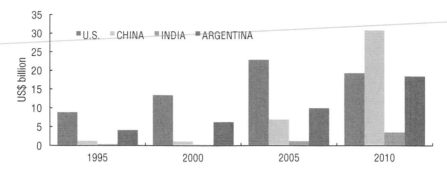

Graph 5B. Chile's Exports to U.S., China, India, and Japan

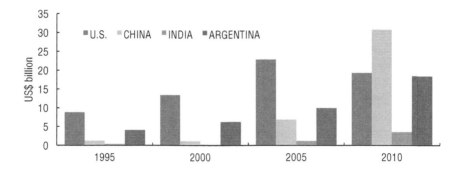

and 2010 India's oil imports from the region came mostly from this country, accounting for almost 37% (2010) of the total purchased by India from South America.

China's imports from the region show more consistency: Brazil and Chile have been China's main sources of imports from South America from 2000 to 2010. These two countries accounted for 70% of all exports by South America to China in 2010 (up from 62% in 2000). But while Brazil's share grew from 34% (2000) to 47% (2010), Chile's fell from 28% (2000) to 22.4% (2010). China's imports from Brazil grew from $ 1.6 billion (2000) to $ 38.1 billion (2010)—a whopping increase of 23.5 times. This enormous surge of Chinese purchases, combined with the economic crisis in the United States, placed China as the #1 destination for Brazilian exports in 2010 (position maintained in 2011) (see Graph 5A). The same happened in Chile, and

Table 1. China Imports From South America: Main Countries and Products

Country	Product	US$ million	% Total
2000			
Brazil	Soy beans	465.82	28.7
	Iron ore	437.63	27.0
	Chemical woodpulp	98.54	6.1
Chile	Copper products	757.97	56.6
	Metal ores (99.6% copper ore)	310.71	23.2
	Chemical woodpulp	159.52	11.9
2010			
Brazil	Iron ore	16,721.76	43.9
	Soy beans	8,148.32	21.4
	Petroleum (crude)	4,231.07	11.1
Chile	Copper products	11,000.96	61.3
	Metal ores (copper ore: $3.9 bi; iron ore: $0.9 bi)	5,068.82	28.3
	Chemical woodpulp	726.91	4.10

3 Main Products

	2000	2010
Brazil	61.80%	76.40%
Chile	91.80%	93.70%

China is now the main destination of its products, displacing its traditional destinations, the United States and Japan (see Graph 5B).

South American exports to China and India are mostly commodities and quite stable in terms of their composition. China's main interest has been in metal ores, soy beans, copper (and copper products) and oil; India's is in oil, copper ore, soy bean oil and cane sugar.

In the case of China's purchases from its main regional partners, Brazil and Chile, there has been an increased concentration of the 3 main products in total amount bought (more in Chile than in Brazil). The three main products imported by China from these two partners alone represented 57.4% of everything bought by China from the region (see Table 1). China's imports of iron ore from Brazil—the most important single product—increased over 38 times; those of soy beans from Brazil 17.5 times, and copper products from Chile almost 15 times.

Table 2. India's Imports from South America—Top 5 Products, 2010

Product	US$ billion	Country	%South America
Oil, crude	4.98	Venezuela	41.48
Copper ore	1.35	Chile	11.25
Oil, crude	1.30	Brazil	10.83
Soy ben oil	0.88	Argentina	7.33
Cane sugar	0.75	Brazil	6.25
Others	2.74	-	22.86
TOTAL	12.00	-	100.00

India's trading pattern even more concentrated than that of China's: Venezuelan crude oil represents 99.7% of all items purchased from that country; copper ore accounted for 86.3% of all Chilean exports to India; and soy bean oil accounted for 84% of all Argentine exports to India (Table 2). Trade with Brazil was more diversified, but the three main products—crude oil, cane sugar and metal ores—still accounted for almost three-fourths of all Indian imports from Brazil.

South American countries have become a growing source of energy for China and India, particularly since the mid-2000s. Between 2000 and 2010, China's energy imports from the region rose from $ 0.1 billion to $ 12.4 billion. Even factoring in the rise in oil prices, South America went from being the origin of 0.6% of China's oil imports in 2000 to 6.5% in 2010. An even more dramatic shift occurred with India: while the region had a practically negligible participation in India's oil purchases from 2000 until 2005—between 0.0005% and 0.015%—in 2006 it rose to 0.93% and by 2010 the weight of South America as an energy source for India also reached 6.5% (Graph 6A and 6B).

Because India's trade volume with South America is much smaller than China's, oil from South America has a much greater weight for the former, representing almost 60% of all Indian imports in 2010 from the region (Graph 7A). So even if China purchases more oil from South America in absolute terms than India, oil is not the focus for China as it is for India.

Graph 6A. China and India: Imports of Energy from South America

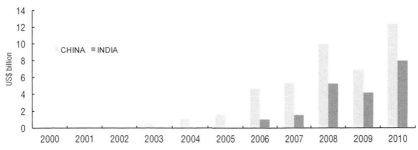

Graph 6B. China and India: Imports of Energy from South America

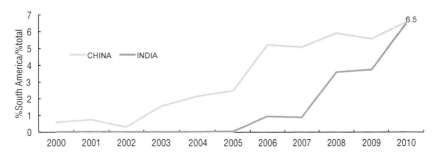

The main source of oil for both has historically been Venezuela, with Brazil coming in second place. It is important to note, however, that even this increase in Chinese and Indian interest in Venezuelan oil does not come close to U.S. oil imports from Venezuela: according to the Energy Information Administration (EIA), while China bought 6% of all oil exported by Venezuela in 2010 and India 5.6%, the U.S. bought 43% of it.

China is increasingly interested in Brazil as a source of oil, within a broader context of diversification of supplies. In 2011 Brazil surpassed Venezuela as China's main source of oil in the region, and China has been entering Brazil's oil sector by acquiring non-controlling stakes in foreign—mostly European—oil companies with existing operations.[11]

---

[11]http://www.latinbusinesschronicle.com/app/article.aspx?id=5401

Graph 7A. China and India: Energy in Total Imports from South America

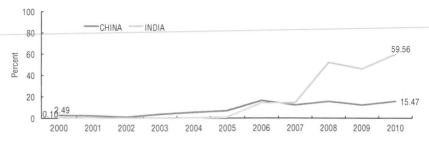

Graph 7B. India: Imports of Energy from South America

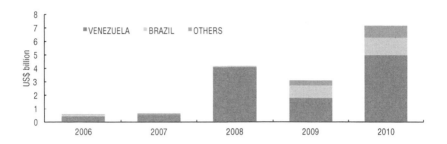

Two points are relevant regarding Indian oil imports. First, they have varied quite a bit, even as Venezuela and Brazil were consistently the most important LAC sources—oscillating between 81% and 98% of all South American oil bought during the period 2006-2010 (Graph 7B). Second, Brazil is an oil exporter and importer. While it exports medium-heavy "sweet" oil (i.e. petroleum with low sulphur level), it imports "light" low-sulphur oil as well as refined (non-crude) oil. With India, Brazil exports crude oil and imports diesel, as Brazil's current refining capacity is insufficient. According to Petrobrás, this will change by 2017, when its new refineries are fully operational. Until then it is likely that Indian diesel will remain a significant portion of Brazil's imports from this country.

With regard to investment in South America, India has a much more modest profile than China's. While the former has invested approximately $12 billion in the region (essentially from private companies), China Development Bank and the Export-Import Bank of China alone are estimated to have extended over $75 billion in credits to Latin American[12] governments—with some $ 46 billion of these in loan commitments that are commodity-backed. The Chinese credit of $37 billion to the region in 2010 was more than the total of credits given by the World Bank, the Inter-American Development Bank and United States Export-Import Bank combined. Also, Indian FDI is much more concentrated on "high end" sectors, such as IT products & services, and pharmaceuticals; China's FDI targets mostly investments in natural resources (e.g. mining, oil). According to the Economic Commission for Latin America and the Caribbean (ECLAC), 90% of China's confirmed investment in Latin America targeted the extraction of natural resources.[13]

As these numbers illustrate, trade between the Asian giants and South America has grown exponentially, to the benefit of all parties. Yet, even a cursory analysis of the composition of this trade shows that it reflects a First World-Third World pattern, with China and India playing First World, and South America that of Third World, i.e. selling raw materials and buying manufactured goods.[14] The fact that the region, on average, enjoys a much higher per capita income than either China or India, makes this type of trading and investment link paradoxical, if not problematic. But before attempting to address this issue, let us turn to Africa. Does the type of economic relationships that China and India have with Africa—particularly Sub-Saharan Africa (SSA)—differ substantially from the one that is apparent in South America, or are they broadly similar?

China and India's Trade with Sub-Saharan Africa

China and India have expanded their trade with Sub-Saharan Africa (SSA) tenfold between 2000 and 2010 (Graph 8). This has led to a greater weight of Africa for their trade balance, although one that is still smaller than that that of South America (see Graph 2). In 2010 China imported almost $80 billion from and exported some $54 billion to South America. With regard to China and Sub-Saharan Africa, the comparable figures are almost $ 60 billion and $44 billion—a pattern that remained in 2011. The inverse happened for India, as its

---

[12]Which here includes also Mexico, Central American and the Caribbean countries.

[13]ECLAC, *Foreign direct Investment in Latin America and the Caribbean 2010.*

[14]See Nicola Phillips, "Coping with China," in Cooper and Heine, *op.cit,* pp. 100-121.

Graph 8. China and India: Trade with Sub-Saharan Africa

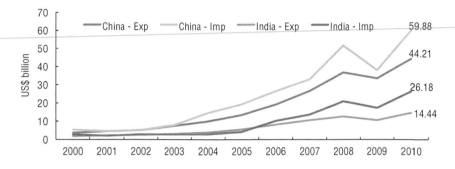

Graph 9A. Sub-Saharan Africa as Destination of China and India's Exports

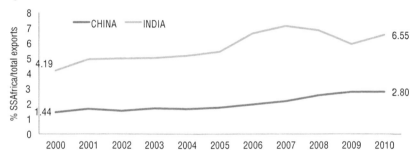

Graph 9B. Sub-Saharan Africa as Source of China and India's Exports

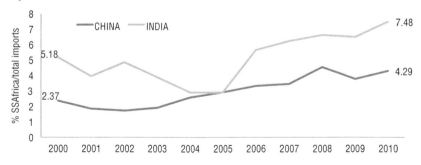

trade with South America is still well below that with SSA. Trade with this sub-region has grown in both countries, but it is more significant for India than for China (Graph 9A and 9B; for South America see graphs 1A and 1B). India also has had a growing trade deficit with SSA

Graph 10A. China: Exports to Sub-Saharan Africa

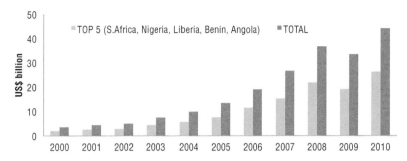

Graph 10B. China: Exports to Sub-Saharan Africa—Top 5 Partners

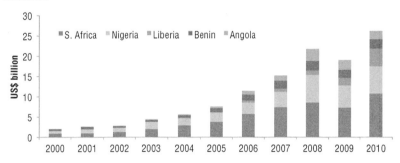

since the mid-2000s; by 2010, its imports from the region were almost double its exports.

Sub-Saharan Africa is made up of 48 independent states,[15] each with its own foreign trade profile. This partially explains some of the variation in trading partners that China and India each have. While both are strongly engaged with South Africa, the continent's strongest and most diversified economy, and the biggest buyer of Chinese and Indian products, these countries have different sets of partners.

South Africa and Nigeria—the subcontinent's top two economies— are the biggest African buyers of Chinese products. While their purchases of Chinese goods have increased steadily, their share of total

---

[15]Following the World Bank's definition, Sub-Saharan Africa comprises all African countries except for: Algeria, Egypt, Libya, Morocco, Tunisia and Western Sahara.

Graph 11A. India: Exports to Sub-Saharan Africa

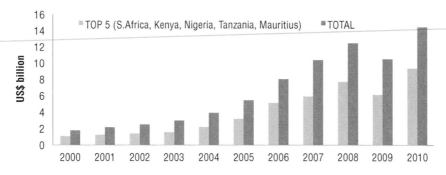

Graph 11B. India: Exports to Sub-Saharan Africa—Top 5 Partners

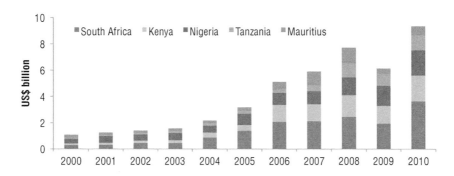

African imports from China has decreased from 43.4% (2000) to 39.6% (2010). Once Liberia, Benin and Angola are added, the participation of the top five partners in total Chinese exports to Africa becomes very stable, varying between 56% and 60% (Graphs 10A and 10B). As in the case of South America, (cheap) manufactured goods account for the bulk of Chinese exports to these countries.

All top five destinations of Indian products in Africa during 2000-2010 were former British colonies: South Africa, Kenya, Nigeria, Tanzania and Mauritius (Graphs 11A and 11B). Their combined weight has changed from 50.2% (2000) to 60% (2010). Indian exports to the region are mostly organic chemicals, pharmaceutical products, diesel, cotton yarn and vehicles.

Graph 12A. China and India: Imports of Energy from Sub-Saharan Africa

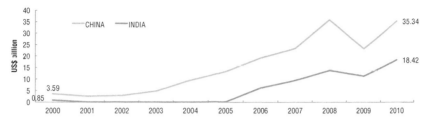

Graph 12B. China and India: Energy in Total Imports from Sub-Saharan Africa

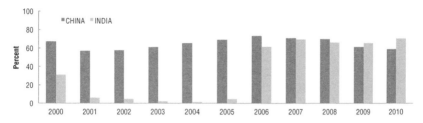

Chinese and Indian imports from Sub-Saharan Africa are largely crude oil and raw materials, indicating the growing importance of the sub-region as an energy source of them. The combined purchases of African energy products[16] from China and India grew from $4.5 billion (2000) to $53.7 billion by the end of the decade (Graph 12A). While India suddenly "woke up" to African oil between 2005-2006, China began a bit earlier (2003-2004). In 2010 18.7% of all energy imported by China and 16.6% by India came from SSA. Since 2007, energy products have represented between 60-70% of all of what was purchased from the region by the two Asian giants (Graph 12B).

Despite the considerable increase in absolute value, the relative weight of African countries as a source of energy products for China remained quite stable—around 20%—between 2004 and 2010 (Graph 13A). But while Africa had a practically negligible participation in

[16]The Harmonized System Commodity Description and Coding System (HS) is the most used international classification system for trade. Every product traded is coded and placed under a specific category. The numbers related to term "energy products" were calculated based on HS Chapter 27 which includes energy derived from fossil fuels and electrical energy.

Graph 13. China and India: Sub-Saharan Africa in Total Imports of Energy

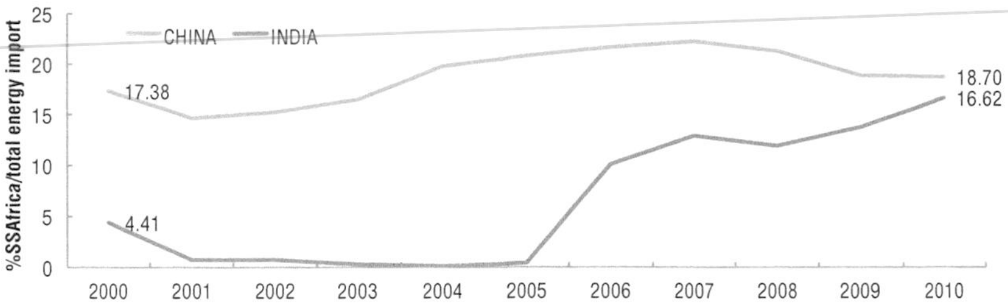

India's total energy purchases from 2001 to 2005 (an average of 0.5%), between 2006 and 2010 it jumped to a much higher level; by 2010 it was the source of one-sixth of India's total energy purchases (Graph 13).

China and India have also diversified their respective sources of African energy. In 2000, China imported energy from 9 African countries, and India from 6. By the end of the decade, 15 countries supplied China and 12 sold to India. China's main sources during 2000-2010 were Angola, Sudan, Congo (Brazzaville), Nigeria South Africa and Equatorial Guinea with an increasing concentration over the period, with these countries responsible for 97% all Chinese oil purchases in SSA. Angola alone has grown steadily in absolute and relative numbers, supplying an average of 63% of Sub-Saharan African oil destined for China (Graphs 14A and 14B), making China the biggest importer of Angolan oil.[17] In fact, since 2005 Angola has been the number two source of Chinese oil after Saudi Arabia. In 2010 Saudia Arabia accounted for 18.9% of China's imported oil and Angola accounted for 16.8%. Sudan has been a stable second source of Chinese Sub-Saharan African oil since 2006, accounting on average for 5% of China's total imported oil. In 2010 China was by far the biggest importer of Sudanese oil,[18] placing Sudan in the top ten sources of

---

[17]Angola did not report to UNCOMTRADE its exports for 2010, so a proxy analysis was done by looking at the countries that reported imports from Angola; given variances in exchange rates, a direct comparison between reporters is not precise.

[18]As in the case of Angola, Sudan did not report to UNCOMTRADE its exports for 2010, so a proxy analysis was done by looking at the countries that reported imports from Sudan; given variances in exchange rates, a direct comparison between reporters is not precise.

Graph 14A. China: Imports of Energy from Sub-Saharan Africa

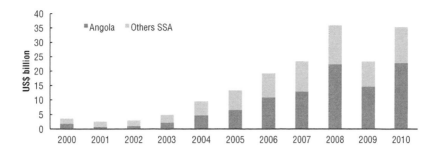

Graph 14B. China: Imports of Energy from Sub-Saharan Africa, Selected Countries

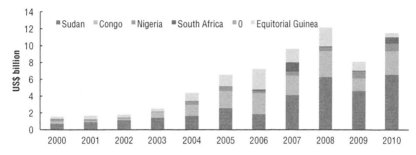

Chinese oil since 2000. In 2010 it represented 4.8% of total Chinese oil imports, ranking #6.

India's main sources of oil in Sub-Saharan Africa have been Nigeria and Angola, which combined were the source of over four-fifths of all oil India bought from the sub-region between 2006 and 2010, followed by South Africa, Sudan and Congo (Graphs 15A and 15B). During this period Nigeria was India's number one partner, although its relative importance has been in decline, falling from a 90.4% share in 2006 to 55% in 2010. Nonetheless, in 2010 India was Nigerian oil's #2 destination, as the Asian country purchased 11% of all Nigerian energy sold, with the U.S. as #1 (37.5%), and China ranking only #19, purchasing less than 1% of all Nigerian oil that year. Because of this high volume from Nigeria to India, this oil-rich country was the second most important source of oil for India (responsible for 11% of Indian oil imports), with Saudi Arabia taking the lead (18.3%). And

Graph 15A. India: Imports of Energy from Sub-Saharan Africa

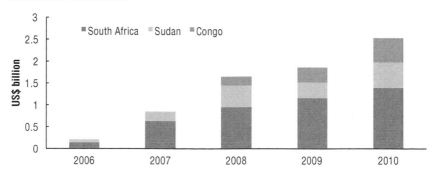

Graph 15B. India: Imports of Energy from Sub-Saharan Africa, Selected Countries

Indian purchases of Angola's oil have increased significantly in absolute and relative terms: from $ 0.18 billion in 2006 to $ 4.8 in 2010; increasing their participation as the source of India's oil imports from SSA from 2.9% in 2006 to 26.2% in 2010. By 2010 India was the third biggest importer of Angolan oil (buying almost 10% of this country's oil) and accounting for 5.4% of all oil purchased from India that year.

Angola, South Africa and Sudan accounted for between two-thirds and three-fourths of all products imported from Sub-Saharan Africa by China throughout the 2000/2010 period. In 2010, Angola accounted for almost 40% of all African purchases, followed by South Africa's 25% and Sudan's 11% (Graphs 16A and 16B).

Out of China's top 5 Sub-Saharan Africa import partners for 2010—Angola, South Africa, Sudan plus Congo and Zambia—it is lit-

Graph 16A. China: Imports from Sub-Saharan Africa

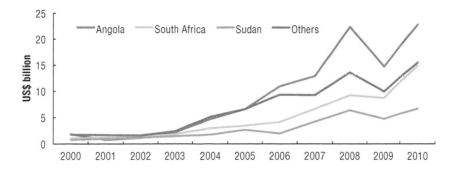

Graph 16B. China: Imports from Sub-Saharan Africa

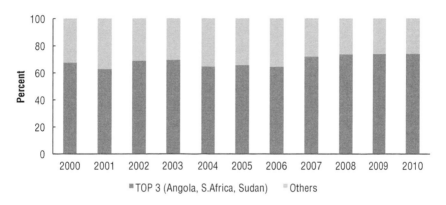

tle surprise that only South Africa exported a (somewhat) diversified list of products. Nonetheless, it was quite concentrated in metal ores, business services[19] and precious metals, with the top three products representing around 70% of all goods imported in 2000 and 2005 and almost 80% in 2010. This same year China was the #1 importer of South African products (11.4%); followed by the U.S. (9.9%), and with India at #6 (4.2%). All other countries were extremely concentrated around a single product: Angola and Sudan's exports to China consist almost 100% of oil (and around 90% for Congo), with Zambia exporting over 90% of only one product: copper.

---

[19]The category "Business Services, unspecified," as indicated by its own name, makes it difficult to allow for a thorough understanding of what these actually were (its HS classification is 999999).

Graph 17A. India: Imports from Sub-Saharan Africa

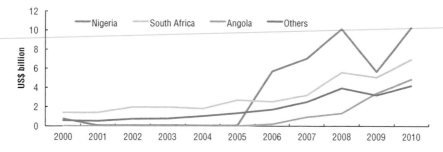

Graph 17B. India: Imports from Sub-Saharan Africa

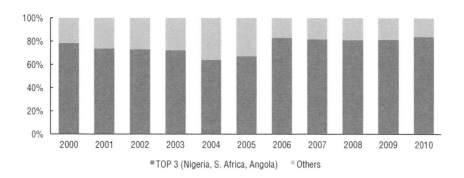

As for India, once all imports of SSA products are included, the top 3 partners were Nigeria, South Africa and Angola, which have accounted for about 82% of goods purchased by this Asian country from the sub-region since 2006. While Indian imports from South Africa grew in the overall period, its relative weight decreased in light of the enormous leap in purchases from Nigeria and Angola by the second half of the decade (graphs 17A and 17B).

Similarly to China, India's most important partners exported (essentially) only a primary commodity such as oil or metals. While Nigeria and Angola sold close to 100% in oil, Indian purchases from South Africa have historically been centered on gold, with energy playing a minor but growing role, here the main product being coal (not oil). In 2010, India was South Africa's sixth largest export market (4.2%).

In the end, most Chinese and Indian foreign energy supplies are still coming from outside of South America and Sub-Saharan Africa: traditional Middle Eastern countries and the closer Asian energy-exporting nations. However, the combined weight of the "new" regions has grown for both China and (particularly) for India since the mid-2000s, with them accounting for roughly one fourth of all energy imported by China and India in 2010 (Graph 18A, 18B and 18C).

Yet, there are differences between China's and India's reliance on South America and Sub-Sahara African countries for their energy needs. The first point to make is that energy does not constitute the focus of China's purchases in South America. Even if its weight has risen from 2.5% (2000) to 15.5% (2010), it still means that about 85% of what China bought from this region was not related to energy (i.e., largely commodities, such as metals and soy beans). Indian imports, on the other hand, have become more focused on energy: between 2008 and 2010, around half of all goods purchased from the region consisted of energy products. As for imports from SSA, energy represents an average of two-thirds of all Indian imports between 2006 and 2010. Another conclusion from the numbers is that China's purchases of energy from SSA between 2000 and 2010 reveal a quite interesting scenario: while it has bought increasingly more energy from the region in absolute terms (graph 14A), the relative increase of non-energy products has been higher since the mid-2000s. While in 2006 almost three-fourths of everything China bought from African countries was related to energy, by 2010 this accounted for slightly less than 60%. In other words, China's import of African primary commodities is growing faster than its energy imports (Graph 19).

Despite frequent concerns expressed about China and India's trade relations with Africa, a recent report found no evidence indicating that the "new players" were hindering the region's industrialisation, debt sustainability or governance.[20] And while Chinese aid to Sub-Sahara African countries is connected to interest in natural resources, other reasons also come into play for decision-making (i.e. politics, ideology, trade)—as does most Western aid to the region.[21] The broader context

---

[20]OECD, *African Economic Outlook*, 2010.

[21]For more on Chinese aid to Africa, see: Brautigam, Deborah (2010), *The Dragon's Gift: the Real Story of China in Africa*, Oxford University Press, New York, NY.

Graph 18A. South America and Sub-Saharan Africa as Energy Sources

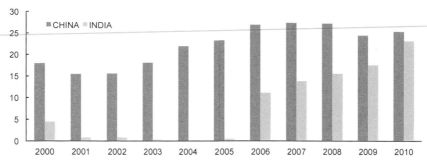

Graph 18B. China's Sources of Energy

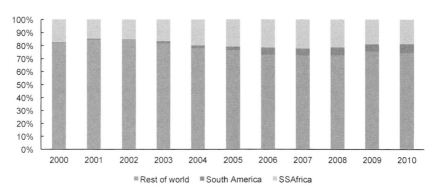

Graph 18C. India's Sources of Energy

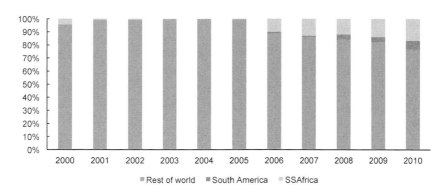

Graph 19. China and India: Importance of Energy Imports

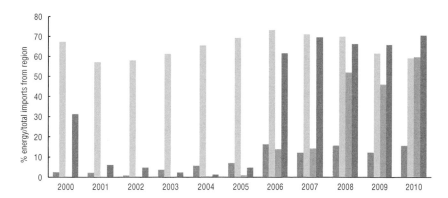

is that China's trade with Sub-Saharan Africa countries has been growing within a decade-long process of increased presence on the continent: by 2002, it displaced Great Britain as the third most important trading partner; four years later, it was #2, surpassing France; and in 2009 it took the first place from the United States. And according to a recent report from the Chinese government, "Africa is likely to surpass the EU and the US to become China's largest trade partner in three to five years."[22]

The surge of Chinese and (to a lesser degree) Indian trade with South American and Sub-Sahara African countries was also influenced by the 2008-2009 financial crisis, one result of which were falling U.S. and European imports not only from these two regions, but from China and India as well. This gave an increased push—particularly to China—to direct it manufactured goods elsewhere. This was compounded by the fact that China's and India's imports from these regions consist mostly of primary commodities. In other words, while the "traditional" buyers bought less of commodities and manufactured goods (from everyone), the "newcomers" interacted with South America and Sub-Saharan Africa, by essentially buying commodities and selling their own manufactured goods and shifting their trade balance pattern. Probably the greatest concern for the countries in the sub-regions is that the flux of cheap manufactured goods from China—

[22]http://www.chinadaily.com.cn/china/2012-10/13/content_15814760.htm

helped by an undervalued *renminbi*—doesn't affect permanently the industries of so many developing countries.

Contrary to what one might have thought, given the differences in levels of social and economic development, the patterns of trade and investment that we see in Africa by China and India share some broad similarities with the ones we find in South America. India, given the lower amount of resources it can mobilize, underscores a bit more the capacity-building dimension of its links with Africa, much as Brazil does. But, by and large, it is access to SSA's natural resources that acts as the main *leitmotiv* behind India's growing presence in the African continent.[23]

Conclusion

The paradox is only too apparent. On the one hand, the two continents in the South Atlantic Basin have had a remarkable first decade in the new century. They have grown at high rates, witnessed considerable progress in democratization (though a lot more on the South American side than on the African one), and stabilized their economies so as to withstand international crises like that of 2008-2009. On the other hand, it could well be argued that this remarkable performance has taken place at a certain cost. It has not been the result of internally-driven, self-consciously made policy choices, but simply the product of the commodities boom of the "naughties," driven by China and India. The danger of this is that, particularly in mining and in oil, these are non-renewable resources that at some point run out. What happens then?

Moreover, the argument has been made that not only do the links with Asia promote mostly, if not exclusively, the primary sector of the SSA and South American economies. They could, in fact, contribute to the "deindustrialization" of these continents. With premium prices

---

[23]On India's presence in Africa, see Ian Taylor "India's rise in Africa," *International Affairs* 88:4 (July 2012), pp. 779-798. See also Fantu Cheru and Cyril Obi, (eds.), *The rise of China and India in Africa*. London: Zed Books, 2010; and Garth Le Pere and Garth Shelton, *China, Africa and South Africa*. Midrand, South Africa; Institute for Global Dialogue, 2007. On the significance of China's presence in Africa for LAC, see Chris Alden, "China y Africa: un espejo distante para América Latina," in *Colombia Internacional* 75 (enero a junio de 2012), pp.19-47.

being paid for minerals and food products, all the incentives are to invest in those activities for export, and import cheap Chinese and Indian finished products in turn. This is not the way forward for self-sustaining, long term development. Both in Sub-Saharan Africa and in South America such export-dependence on commodities is not healthy and demands greater efforts to diversify export baskets and add more value to goods sold abroad, what has been referred to as "the second phase of export-led development."

One way out of this predicament is for African and South American industries to access the Asian value chains that contribute so much to global manufacturing output these days. Another is to start "looking sideways," as it were, and to explore the manner in which the sub-regions could work together to complement their economies, across the Atlantic and in so doing, laying the foundations for a newly invigorated and resurgent South Atlantic Basin. The lead role that Brazil has taken in kick-starting this ambitious but potentially highly rewarding process is perhaps an indicator that this is by no means an unrealistic project.

Chapter 5

The Impact of TTIP on Brazil

Vera Thorstensen and Lucas Ferraz[1]

The world is facing a significant transformation process supported by new paradigms: revolutionary innovations in all fronts, new information technologies, huge and speedy mobility of capital, invention of risky financial tools, and globalization of production. The impact of these phenomena on trade and trade activities is strong and drastic, leaving not much time for the postponement of decisions.

The trading system is facing serious challenges caused by these transformations: difficulty in concluding the 15-year-old multilateral negotiation at the World Trade Organization (WTO); the multiplication of preferential trade agreements (PTAs); and the necessity to reinvent trade rules used to support global value chains.

Given the difficulties encountered in the Doha Round to adapt old trade rules to new reality, the United States and the European Union (EU) decided to launch a new profile of PTAs, including mega-regional trade agreements such as the TTIP (Transatlantic Trade and Investment Partnership) and the TPP (Trans-Pacific Partnership), encompassing half of world trade.

More than the reduction of tariffs, these mega-regional agreements aim to define a new structure and new modalities for all kinds of non-tariff barriers to trade, along with new rules for important trade-related issues such as investment and competition, and new concerns as environment, climate, labor, food scarcity, animal welfare, privacy standards and mounting consumer pressure.

Brazil, as a global but relatively small international trader, has opted for giving priority to the multilateral track, where it assumed it could influence the game and better defend its interests. However, the conclusion of the Doha Round is more difficult to achieve than expected.

[1]The authors would like to thank their research team members Carolina Müller, Rodolfo Cabral, Belisa Eleoterio, and Thiago Nogueira.

115

Moreover, most countries have chosen another path: to increase their trade through negotiations of PTAs. On the one hand, this strategy creates new market opportunities. On the other hand, it results in the fragmentation of international trade regulation, creating conflicts and lack of transparency.

Nonetheless, this new reality must be confronted. The EU is changing its priorities from the WTO and smaller PTAs and has opted for a new challenge—a negotiation with its most controversial trade partner, the United States. The creation of the TTIP is a revolutionary initiative for the trading system. It will surely benefit the two parties to the negotiation. But at the same time it will create an uncertain scenario for all other trade partners, because, due to its size, it will establish a new system of rules, probably in conflict with the WTO because it will discriminate between elements that are included and elements that are excluded from this PTA. New rules will occur in areas expanding WTO rules (WTO-plus), such as services and intellectual property, but rules will also be generated in new areas, such as environment, climate change, labor, investment and competition (WTO-extra rules).

A study of current TTIP proposals demonstrates quite clearly that the main focus of this agreement will be on the elimination of non-tariff barriers and the creation of better regulatory coherence. The most import proclaimed achievement will be the construction of the 21st century trading system. For outsiders, this raises concerns regarding the role to be played by the WTO.

The Growth of Preferential Trade Agreements

International trade is undergoing significant and complex change that represents a great challenge to Brazilian foreign trade policy. The deadlock in multilateral negotiations under the WTO Doha Round has led major players in international trade, notably the United States and the European Union, to focus on the negotiation of preferential trade agreements (PTAs), where they could advance trade rules, lower trade barriers and promote integration with their partners, signaling the rules they want for the present century.

Figure 1. Preferential Trade Agreements Notifications (1948-2012)

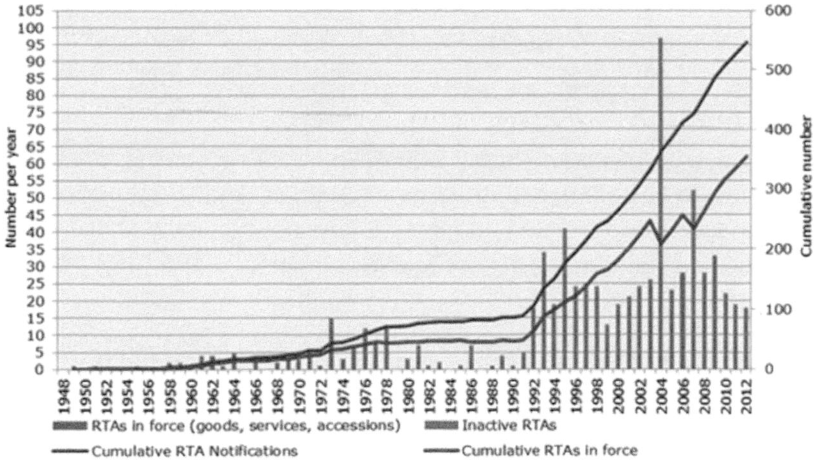

Source: WTO Secretariat.

Figure 1 shows that there has been a huge increase in the number of Preferential Trade Arrangements (PTAs) in the past years, pointing to the importance that these agreements have acquired in the regulation of international trade flows.

The first generation of PTAs sought to reduce or eliminate tariffs in goods between partners. This preferential access could either increase international trade flows, due to the market liberalization promoted by the agreement (trade creation) or to divert flows from more competitive players (trade diversion).

The following generation of PTAs has promoted, besides tariff reductions, the negotiation of rules on subjects not fully dealt by the multilateral system, establishing a relevant framework of trade regulation on the regional level, that affected not only the partners of the respective PTA, but also influenced multilateral negotiations.

The current generation of PTAs keeps the trends of the previous agreements, but in a deeper process. These deep-integration PTAs promote a greater coordination and harmonization between trade partners, facilitating the establishment of production chains on the regional level, contributing to the major phenomenon of trade in the 21st century: global value chains. The TTIP between the EU and the United States, and the TPP between the United States, Australia, Brunei, Canada, Chile, Japan, Malaysia, Mexico, New Zealand, Peru, Singapore, and Vietnam, are the most ambitious negotiations of these last generation PTAs.

The negotiations of these two agreements present an ambitious agenda, with substantial elimination of tariffs in goods, enlargement of market access in services and government procurement, harmonization and mutual recognition of technical, sanitary and phytosanitary measures.

Besides ambitious schedules of preferential tariffs, modern PTAs have a broad regulatory framework to deal with bilateral international trade flows of goods and services. This set of rules deals with several trade-related activities and may have a direct impact on market access of the preferential trade partners. These rules, whether WTO-plus or WTO-extra, often surpass the scope of the agreements of the multilateral trading system, and encompass themes not regulated by the WTO.

This proliferation of PTAs, with rules that promote deep integration between partners, has an important effect on international trade flows, since countries that participate in these agreements have a wider market access, provided both by the reduction of tariff and non-tariff barriers, as well as harmonization of trade rules, trade facilitation, and other factors. Yet countries that do not participate in any PTA tend to suffer losses in their share of exports to other countries, because products from preferential partners have a preferential access, and can be more competitive when enjoying the benefits conferred by the PTA.

Preferential Trade Agreements and Brazil

For many years Brazil has prioritized multilateral negotiations in detriment of preferential ones. The rationale behind this option was that the country would have greater bargaining power if negotiating in the multilateral forum together with other developing countries. But with the stalemate of the Doha Round, Brazil needs to change its strategy and reformulate its trade policy. Two priorities deserve deep discussion: the participation of Brazil in new PTAs and the participation of Brazil in a world of global value chains. Immobilization will result in the isolation of Brazil in international trade.

A relevant issue for the Brazilian agricultural sector will be the negotiation by the EU of preferential tariff quotas to the United States. These quotas shall impact and reduce the global tariff quotas offered by the EU in its agricultural market and can significantly harm Brazilian exports.

In addition, the enlargement of market access of the trade partners participating in these two agreements shall have as an effect not only the increase in trade flows between these parties, but can also reduce flows from other players such as Brazil to these destinations (trade diversion), since Brazilian products will not face this privilege market access.

The agreements will also include several WTO-plus and WTO-extra rules such as enhanced intellectual property protection, as proposed by the United States in the TPP, regulation of e-commerce, competition rules, liberalization and protection of investments, regulation of trade related aspects of state owned enterprises, provisions on small and medium sized enterprises, rules of international supply chains, amongst other themes.[2] One major concern in the development of WTO-plus rules in PTAs is that they will eventually affect all trade player and not only the ones that have directly participated in the negotiation of the PTA.

The rules of deep integration negotiated within those agreements, which regulate behind the border barriers, such as technical regulations and intellectual property, are likely to be extended to all other players, since these rules imply in a modification of the countries' national legislation to be applied to all goods or services trade within the territory of the respective country. Therefore, Brazilian products are likely to face technical and sanitary standards negotiated within the TTIP or enhanced intellectual property protection in patents registered in any of the TPP partners, which may also damage Brazilian exports.

---

[2]Fergusson, I., Cooper, W., Jurenas, R., and Williams, B., *The Trans-Pacific Partnership Negotiations and Issues for Congress*, Congressional Research Service Report for Congress, June 2013, pp. 47-48; and *Interim Report to Leaders from the Co-Chairs EU-US High Level Working Group on Jobs and Growth*, June 2012.

Brazil will have to adapt to several of the requirements present in these two agreements without having participated in the drafting such rules, and thus, without being able to advance its own interests and perspectives in the regulation of such themes. Therefore, if the country does not participate in this movement of negotiation of 21st century PTAs, it will become a rule-taker instead of a rule-maker, bearing all the costs related to its late arrival to this new generation of international trade rules.

The TPP and the TTIP are likely to promote much deeper economic integration among their respective members, resulting in the elimination of several trade barriers, regulatory harmonization, and creation of regional value chains. The benefits of this deep integration include an increase in business opportunities (trade in goods and services and investments) among the partners as well as the exchange of know-how and technology through the internationalized production chain, enhancing the countries' competitiveness and negatively affecting trade partners that do not participate in this process of regional integration.

This chapter presents simulations that show the costs of Brazil's isolation. Assuming that Brazil does not sign any PTA with significant trade partners, and that the TTIP enters into force, this chapter presents the impact of these agreements on Brazil's productive sectors and its main macroeconomic variables.

Brazil's Trade Profile with Selected Partners

In 2012, Brazil's international trade was valued at $465.7 billion, a decrease of 3.4% compared to the previous year's total of $482.2 billion (see Table 1). Brazilian exports in 2012 were valued at $242.6 billion, a decline of 5.3% from the previous year. Imports were valued at $223.1 billion, a drop of 1.4% from the previous year. Notwithstanding the decrease observed in the period, if one considers the volume of exports, the variation in comparison to 2011 presents a modest reduction of 0.3%.

The main destinations of Brazilian exports are: China, with a share of 17.0% of all Brazilian exports; the United States with 11.1%; Argentina with a 7.4%; the Netherlands with 6.2%; and Japan with 3.3%. The EU accounts for 20.1% of all Brazilian exports.

Table 1. Brazil: Trade Balance ($ billion)

	2008	2009	2010	2011	2012
Exports	197.9	153.0	201.9	256.0	242.5
Imports	173.2	127.6	181.7	226.2	223.1
Trade Flow	371.1	281.0	383.6	482.2	465.7

Source: SECEX/MDIC.

Table 2. Brazil: Exports to the United States and the EU (2008-2012)

	U.S.		EU		Total	
	$ billion	%1	$ billion	%1	US$ billion	%1
2008	27.4	9.4	46.4	14.76	197.9	23.21
2009	15.6	-43.1	34.0	-26.6	153.0	-22.7
2010	19.3	23.8	43.1	26.7	201.9	32.0
2011	25.8	33.7	52.9	22.7	256.0	26.8
2012	26.7	3.5	48.9	-7.7	242.6	-5.26

Source: SECEX/MDIC. 1%: Variation related to the previous year.

Table 3. Brazil: Share of Exports (%)

	U.S.	EU
2008	13.9	23.4
2009	10.2	22.3
2010	9.6	21.4
2011	10.1	20.7
2012	11.0	20.1

Source: SECEX/MDIC.

The main sources of Brazilian imports are: China, with a share of 15.4% of all Brazilian imports; the United States with 14.6%; Argentina with a 7.4% share; Germany with 6.4%; and Korea with 4.1%. The EU accounts for 21.4% of all Brazilian imports.[3]

Considering exports for the United States and the EU, it is possible to infer Brazilian exports to the EU rose modestly by 5.4% over the past five years, while exports to the United States fell by 3.6% (see Table 2).

Regarding Brazilian exports, one can notice that the participation of the United States (from 13.9% in 2008 to 11% in 2012) and the

---

[3]Cf. SECEX/MDIC.

Figure 2. Brazil: Foreign Trade—Exports (2008-2012)

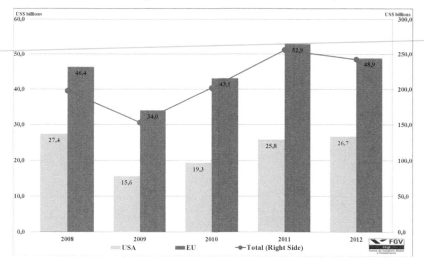

Source: SECEX/MDIC. Elaborated by CGTI.

EU (from 23.4% in 2008 to 20.1% in 2012) were reduced by approximately 3%.

Analyzing Brazilian imports during the 2008-2012 period, it is possible to conclude that imports from the United States rose by 26.6% and imports from the EU rose by 31.8% (see Table 4).

It is worth noting that the average share of these partners in Brazilian imports was maintained during the period of 2008 to 2012 (U.S.: 14.9/14.5% and EU: 20.9/21.4 (see Table 5).

Table 4. Brazil: Imports from the United States and the EU (2008-2012)

	U.S.		EU		Total	
	$ billion	%1	$ billion	%1	US$ billion	%1
2008	25.6	36.9	36.2	35.3	173.0	43.4
2009	20.0	-21.8	29.2	-19.2	127.7	-26.2
2010	27.0	35.0	39.1	33.9	181.8	42.3
2011	34.0	25.6	46.4	18.7	226.2	24.5
2012	32.4	-4.8	47.7	2.7	223.1	-1.4

Source: SECEX/MDIC. 1%: Variation related to the previous year.

Table 5. Brazil: Share of Imports (%)

	U.S.	EU
2008	14.9	20.9
2009	15.7	22.9
2010	14.9	21.5
2011	15.0	20.5
2012	14.5	21.4

Source: SECEX/MDIC.

It is possible to conclude that both imports and exports have increased since 2008. While trade shrank in 2009, the period of the worldwide economic crisis, there was an economic upturn in 2010, and trade flows recovered (see Figure 3).

Brazil-EU Trade

Although the EU has remained Brazil's major trade partner, bilateral trade in the period 2008-2012 demonstrates that the world economic crisis of 2008-2009 influenced both exports and imports from the EU. In 2010 and 2011, there was an increase in bilateral trade flows but in the following period the there was another decline. Nevertheless, Brazilian's trade balance with the EU remains positive.

Figure 3. Brazil: Foreign Trade—Imports (2008-2012)

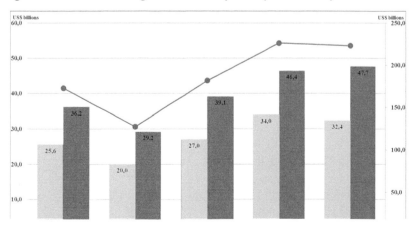

Source: SECEX/MDIC. Elaborated by CGTI.

Figure 4. Brazil-EU Trade (2008-2012)

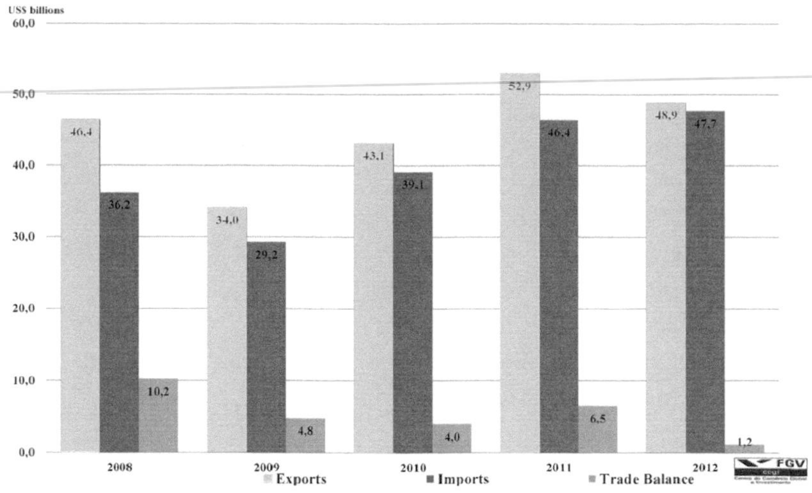

US$ billions

Source: SECEX/MDIC. Elaborated by CGTI.

In 2012, Brazil was the 10th largest source of EU imports, having a share of 2.1% of European total imports; and the eighth major destination of EU exports, with a share of 2.3% of European total exports. On the other hand, the EU is Brazil's leading trading partner, accounting for 19.2% of its total trade flow in 2012 (see Figures 4 and 5).

Brazil's exports to the EU are dominated by primary products, in particular agricultural products (43.5%), and fuels and mining products (28.4%), which corresponded, in 2012, to a share of 71.9% of its total exports to EU. In the same year, manufactures accounter for 24.4% of Brazilian exports to the EU. The most exported manufactured products were machinery and transport equipment (8.6%), chemicals (6.9%), and iron and steel (3.3%).

Approximately 40% of Brazilian exports to the EU consists of agricultural products (AMA); 60% consists of non-agricultural products (NAMA). In 2012, Brazilian AMA products have obtained a 1.0% share of the EU market, making Brazil the single biggest exporter of agricultural products to the EU, while its NAMA products have attained only a 1.3% market share.

Figure 5. Brazil-EU: Foreign Trade Variation and Share (2008-2012)

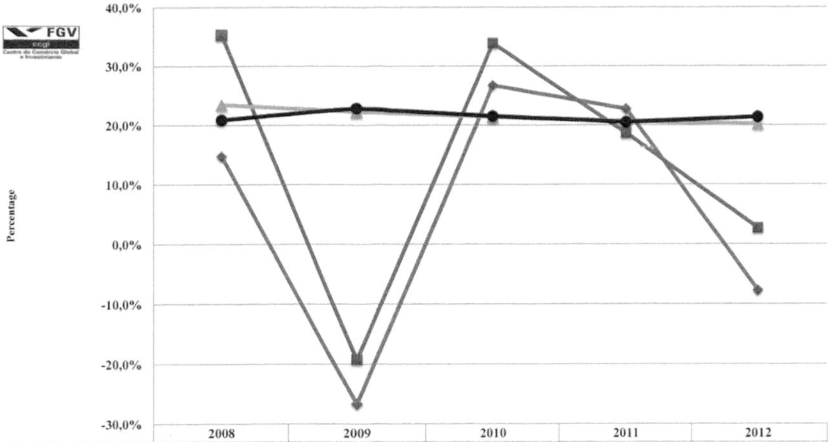

	2008	2009	2010	2011	2012
Exports (Variation)	14,8%	-26,6%	26,7%	22,7%	-7,7%
Imports (Variation)	35,3%	-19,2%	33,9%	18,7%	2,7%
Exports (Share)	23,4%	22,3%	21,4%	20,7%	20,1%
Imports (Share)	20,9%	22,9%	21,5%	20,5%	21,4%

Source: SECEX/MDIC. Elaborated by CGTI.

In contrast, Brazilian imports from the EU consist mostly of manufactured products (83.6% in 2012), especially machinery and transport equipment (45%), and chemicals (22.2%). In goods, Brazil runs an overall trade surplus with the EU, but has a trade deficit in commercial services trade.

Brazil-U.S. Trade

Bilateral trade between Brazil and the United States fell during the economic crisis of 2008-2009. Although Brazilian exports to the United States increased again in 2010, the overall flows had not yet recovered from the crisis, and Brazil's trade balance still operates in deficit (see Figures 6 and 7).

Brazil was the seventh largest destination of U.S. exports in 2012, and accounted for 2.8% of overall U.S. exports that year.[4] The main categories were machinery ($7.7 billion), mineral fuel ($7.2 billion), aircraft ($6.1 billion), electrical machinery ($4.8 billion), and optic and

---

[4]USTR. *Brazil. Available at: http://www.ustr.gov/countries-regions/americas/brazil.*

Figure 6. Brazil-U.S. Trade (2008-2012)

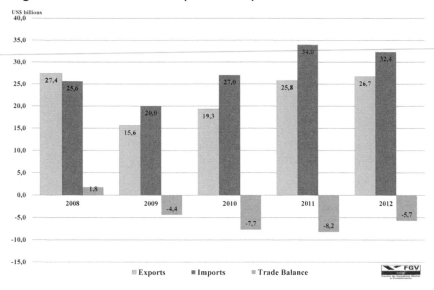

Source: SECEX/MDIC. Elaborated by CGTI.

medical instruments ($2.2 billion). Brazilian imports of agricultural products from the United States totaled $515 million in 2012. The main categories included dairy products ($72 million), snack foods ($21 million), and feeds and fodders ($18 million).

Brazil was also the 15th largest source of U.S. imports in 2012, accounting for just 1.4% of overall U.S. imports that year. But the United States was the third leading source of Brazil's imports, accounting for 14.6% of total Brazilian imports. The United States was also the third major destination of Brazilian exports, accounting for an 11.1% share.[5]

The five largest categories of Brazilian exports to the United States in 2012 were mineral fuel and crude oil ($9.4 billion), iron and steel ($3.5 billion), machinery ($2.7 billion), special other (returns and repairs) ($1.9 billion), and beverages ($1.5 billion). Brazilian exports of agricultural products to the United States totaled $3.4 billion in 2012, making the country the 6th largest supplier of U.S. agricultural

---

[5]Considering all EU members as a single partner.

Figure 7. Brazil-U.S.: Foreign Trade Variation and Share (2008-2012)

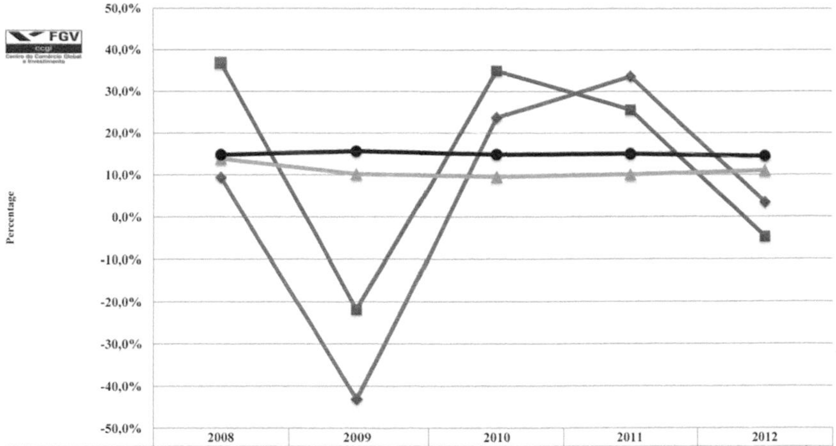

	2008	2009	2010	2011	2012
Exports (Variation)	9,4%	-43,1%	23,8%	33,7%	3,5%
Imports (Variation)	36,9%	-21,8%	35,0%	25,6%	-4,8%
Exports (Share)	13,9%	10,2%	9,6%	10,1%	11,0%
Imports (Share)	14,9%	15,7%	14,9%	15,0%	14,5%

Source: SECEX/MDIC. Elaborated by CGTI.

imports. Leading categories included coffee (unroasted) ($1.3 billion), tobacco ($313 million), fruit and vegetable juices ($242 million), and coarse grains ($227 million).

Trade Barriers

International trade flows may be restrained by different types of barriers: tariffs, technical barriers, sanitary and phytosanitary measures, trade defense instruments, rules of origin, etc. GATT and WTO rounds of multilateral trade negotiations aimed to reduce such barriers, through the negotiation and reduction of bound tariffs in each country's schedule of concessions and through the creation of rules on non-tariff barriers, such as the Agreement on Technical Barriers to Trade, Agreement on Sanitary and Phytosanitary Measures, Agreement on Subsidies and Countervailing Measures, Anti-dumping Agreement and the Agreement on Rules of Origin. These agreements established rules on how non-tariffs barriers could be implemented by members, in order to reduce the use of measures that distorted international trade.

PTAs aim to reduce and restrain even further the applied tariffs and the use of measures that represent barriers to bilateral trade. Through the negotiation of rules in a series of themes, preferential partners can achieve a wider market access because exports face less barriers when entering the preferential market, thus increasing trade flows and economic integration.

Since U.S. and EU tariffs are already relatively low, the main focus of TTIP negotiations will be the reduction and potential alimination of non-tariff barriers, specially technical, sanitary and phytosanitary barriers that represent the most relevant obstacles to bilateral trade.

Trade Barriers in the United States. In accordance with WTO Tariff Profile, the United States hold a simple average MFN tariff of 5.0% for agricultural products and a simple average of 3.3% for non-agricultural products. However, group sectors analyzed separately show some peaks in U.S. tariffs: simple average MFN applied tariff for dairy products is of 19.1%, for sugar and confectionery of 16.6%, and for beverages and tobacco of 15.4%. When it comes to non-agricultural products, the United States applies low tariffs, with higher averages in some sectors, such as 11.4% for clothing and 7.9% for textiles.[6]

The main barriers for exports to the United States include tariff barriers, such as on fruit juices, textiles and apparel; tariff rate quotas for sugar, bovine meat *in natura*, tobacco, and some dairy products; tariff escalation measures on soy oil, which are harmful to Brazilian products; non-tariff measures such as non-recognition of Brazilian conformity procedures; sanitary and phytosanitary barriers; "Buy America" and related provisions; agricultural subsidies; its "blenders credit" incentive program to export biofuels to the EU, thereby negatively affecting Brazilian exports to the EU; antidumping duties on Brazilian producers; ownership requirements in the transportation sector. The United States suspended an additional tariff on ethanol imports, but there is concern in Brazil that pressure is mounting for its return.[7]

---

[6]WTO, *World Tariff Profiles—the United States*, 2012.

[7]As identified by WTO Committees, Reports and Disputes, data provided by SECEX/MDIC and APEX-Brazil, the World Bank, Mercosur, USTR, the U.S. International Trade Commission and the EU.

Trade Barriers in the European Union. In accordance with WTO Tariff Profiles, the European Union holds a simple average MFN tariff of 13.9% for agricultural products and a simple average of 4.0% for non-agricultural products. However, group sectors analyzed separately show much higher averages in specific agricultural sectors. Simple average MFN applied tariff for dairy products is 55.2%, for sugar and confectionery 29.1%, and for animal products 23.0%. When it comes to non-agricultural products, the European Union applies low tariffs, with higher averages for the sectors of clothing (11.5%) and textiles (6.6%).

The main barriers for export to the EU include tariffs on biofuels, bovine meat, chicken, pork, sugar and tobacco, and a rather inpenetrable system of tariffs on food products generally; a discriminatory bananas trading regime; duties as high as 14% on flat panel computer monitors, multifunction printers, and certain cable, satellite, and other set-top boxes; differences between member state implementation and enforcement of EU regulations; strict regulations regarding Genetically Modified Organisms (GMOs); EU climate change regulations; nontransparent procedures and lack of meaningful stakeholder input into policies related to pharmaceutical pricing and reimbursement; subsidies for agriculture and aircraft; EU content requirement for foreign suppliers in such sectors as water, energy, urban transport and postal services; and strict data privacy regulations and legal liability for companies doing business over the internet in the EU.[8]

Trade Barriers in Brazil. Brazil holds a simple average MFN tariff of 10.3% for agricultural products and a simple average of 14.2% for non-agricultural products. Brazil also reveals some higher averages for specific sectors. Brazil applies a simple average MFN tariff of 18.5% for dairy products, 17.2% for beverages and tobacco; and 16.5% for sugar and confectionery, amongst agricultural products. On non-agricultural products, Brazil applies relatively high tariffs, which is also verified frequently in other developing countries. Thus, for instance, simple average MFN tariff is of 35.0% for clothing, 23.3% for textiles and 18.3% for transport equipment.

---

[8]As supported by evidence from WTO Committees, Reports and Disputes, data provided by SECEX/MDIC and APEX-Brazil, the World Bank, Mercosur, the European Commission, the Directorate-General for Trade and the USTR.

Major Brazilian commercial barriers include relatively high tariffs across a wide range of sectors, including automobiles, automotive parts, information technology and electronics, chemicals, plastics, industrial machinery, steel, and textiles and apparel; restrictions on wheat imports, contravening its Uruguay Round commitments; a complex domestic tax system; lack of transparency surrounding import license requirements; a regulation mandating that testing of telecommunications products can only be performed within Brazil; import bans on U.S. and EU live cattle, beef, and beef products; use of indirect taxes to afford protection to Brazilian manufacturers against imports in sectors such as electronics and telecommunication equipment; export restrictions on raw materials; a range of government subsidies and services barriers.

TTIP and Brazil

This chapter analyzes TTIP's implications for Brazil by considering four different hypotheses. The first considers the effects on Brazil of a TTIP that only reduces U.S.-EU tariff barriers. The second considers the effects of tariff reduction plus a partial reduction of non-tariff barriers. The third examines the implications of a complete reduction of these barriers. A final "audacious" alternative is assumed in which Brazil participates in the TTIP under both a partial reduction of agricultural tariffs by the U.S. and EU markets, and under a full liberalization of their agricultural markets.[9]

Simulation 1—Impact of TTIP on Brazil

This simulation presents the impact of the TTIP negotiations on the Brazilian economy. Three different hypotheses are proposed: (i) a full tariff reduction between the United States and the EU; (ii) full tariff elimination plus a 50% reduction of non-tariff barriers (NTB); and (iii) full elimination of both tariffs and NTBs.

Results. Under the first hypothesis—full tariff reduction only between the United States and the EU—Brazilian exports to the

---

[9]The methodology used to estimate non-tariff barriers was adopted from Ecorys, *Non-Tariff Measures in EU-US Trade and Investment—An Economic Analysis*, Report prepared for the European Commission, 2009, http://trade.ec.europa.eu/doclib/docs/2009/december/tradoc_145613.pdf

United States and the EU fall by 0.6%, a decrease of of $0.4 billion. Brazilian imports from the United States and the EU would fall by 0.4%, a decrease of $0.3 billion.

Under the second hypothesis—full U.S.-EU tariff elimination plus a 50% reduction of U.S.-EU non-tariff barriers (NTB), the most probable scenario—Brazil's exports to the United States and the EU fall by 5%, a decrease of $3.8 billion. Brazilian imports from the United States and the EU would fall by 4%, a decrease of $3.1 billion.

Under the third hypothesis—full elimination of both U.S.-EU tariffs and NTBs—Brazil's exports to the United States and the EU fall by 10%, a decrease of $7.8 billion. Brazilian imports from the United States and the EU would fall by 8%, a decrease of $6.4 billion.

These comparisons indicate the opportunities lost to Brazil by remaining outside such negotiations. In addition, since a TTIP agreement is likely to boost U.S. and EU competitiveness and spark additional U.S. and EU exports, Brazil's overall share of world trade is likely to decline.

The simulation also presents differing results for particular sectors.

TTIP results in small losses for most of Brazil's agricultural sectors, with a slightly better scenario according to the level of liberalization of NTBs. One factor that should affect Brazilian agricultural exports to the EU is that any preferential tariff quotas offered by the EU to the United States should affect other countries' market access to the EU, since the global tariff quotas will be shared by many partners, with the United States benefiting from a larger share of such a global quotas. The simulation indicates that Brazilian agriciltures would benefit from the elimination of U.S-EU NTBs.

For Brazilian industry, TTIP results are mixed, with in gains for a number of sectors and losses for others. This can be explained by the fact that the increase of trade flows and economic integration between the EU and the United States would create some demand for exports from other countries as well.

When the elimination of U.S.-EU non-tariff barriers is taken into account, the negative impact to Brazil is more significant with regard to sectoral GDP and trade flows. The trade gains of TTIP will be obtained less through tariff negotiations than through negotiations of non-tariff barriers, including technical barriers, sanitary and phytosanitary measures, trade facilitation, among others, which nowadays are the real barriers to trade.

Considering only the elimination of only tariff barriers in the TTIP, the simulation shows that the impacts to Brazil are negative, but not too significant, representing:

(i)   losses of around 1% in GDP in 16 agrobusiness sectors of 20 sectors considered.

(ii) losses of around 1% in GDP in 9 industrial sectors of 21 sectors considered.

(iii)   losses in the trade balance in 14 agrobusiness sectors of 20 sectors considered, mainly coffee, meat and meat products.

(iv) losses in the trade balance in 8 industrial sectors of 21 sectors considered, mainly leather products, non-metallic products, and motor vehicles and components.

Under the hypothesis of tariff elimination and a 50% reduction on NTB, the results are:

(i)   losses of 1%–3% in GDP in 15 agrobusiness sectors of 20 sectors considered.

(ii) losses of 1%–2% in GDP in 14 industrial sectors of 21 sectors considered.

(iii) losses in the trade balance in 14 agrobusiness sectors of 20 sectors considered, mainly soya, animal feed, coffee, meat and meat products.

(iv) losses in the trade balance in 8 industrial sectors of 21 sectors considered, mainly leather products, non-metallic products, motor vehicles and components, and transport material.

Simulation 2—Impact of Brazil's participation in TTIP on the Brazilian economy

This "audacious" simulation presents the impact to the Brazilian economy of a hypothetical participation of the country in the TTIP negotiations.

The hypothesis assumed for such participation are: (i) a full liberalization of both tariff and NTBs; (ii) a 50% reduction of tariffs in agriculture for the United States and the EU and a full liberalization of all other tariffs and NTBs; and (iii) a 50% liberalization of the EU and U.S. agricultural sectors, 50% liberalization of Brazil's industry and services and a full liberalization of non-tariff barriers for all partners.

When Brazil adheres to the TTIP, its exports register a significant increase:

(i)   a full liberalization of tariffs and NTBs for TTIP results in a strong increase of 126% of Brazilian exports, corresponding to a $95.4 billion raise.

(ii) a 50% reduction of agricultural tariffs plus a full liberalization of all other tariffs and NTBs results in an increase of 102% of the country's exports, corresponding to $77.3 billion.

(iii) a 50% reduction of EU and U.S. agricultural tariffs, a 50% reduction of Brazilian industrial tariffs and a full liberalization of non-tariff barriers for all partners, boost Brazilian exports by 121%, corresponding to $91.5 billion.

(iv) finally, in a more realistic scenario of 50% reduction of EU and U.S. agricultural tariffs, a 50% reduction of Brazilian industrial tariffs and a 50% reduction of non-tariff barriers for all partners, Brazilian exports increase by 67.6%, corresponding to $51.1 billion.[10]

In the TTIP, there is a very expressive increase in the exports of agricultural products, which explains the gains in the land value and the valorization of the Brazilian real.

Regarding imports, when Brazil participates in the TTIP:

(i)   full liberalization of tariffs and NTBs results in an increase of 54% increase in Brazilian imports from the United States and the EU, a $43.1 billion rise.

(ii) a 50% liberalization in agricultural tariffs and a full liberalization in other tariffs and NTBs results in a 46.5% increase in Brazilian imports from the United States and the European Union, a rise of $37.2 billion.

---

[10]Values from Secex (US$ F.O.B.) for 2012.

(iii) a 50% liberalization of the U.S. and EU agricultural sectors, a 50% liberalization in the Brazilian industrial sector and a full liberalization of non-tariff barriers for all partners results in a 34.9% increase in Brazilian imports from the United States and the EU, a rise of $27.9 billion.

(iv) finally, in a more realistic scenario of 50% reduction of EU and U.S. agricultural tariffs, a 50% reduction of Brazilian industrial tariffs and a 50% reduction of non-tariff barriers for all partners, Brazilian imports from the United States and the EU increase by 52.9%, a rise of $ 42.3 billion.[11]

The second simulation also presents different results for particular sectors of the economy.

Assuming Brazilian participation in TTIP, there are highly expressive gains for the majority of Brazil's agricultural sectors in all three scenarios. This presents the greatest opportunity costs of Brazil remaining outside the transatlantic integration process.

The impact on Brazilian industry is mixed, with both losses and gains, partly due to the impact of exchange rates.

The audacious hypothesis of including Brazil as a part of TTIP presents a substantial gain for Brazilian agriculture, but as expected, losses for several of Brazil's industrial sectors due to the overvaluation of exchange rates and the consequent increase of industrial imports. To make this hypothesis viable, two important tasks are needed: the Brazilian industry must face arduous work to improve its competitiveness, and the Brazilian government should also play its role through active economic policies.

In summary:

(i)   gains from 3% to more than 4% in GDP in 13 agrobusiness sectors of 20 sectors considered.

(ii) losses of 1% to 3% in GDP in 19 industrial sectors of 21 sectors considered.

---

[11]Values from Secex (US$ F.O.B.) for 2012.

(iii) gains in the trade balance in 13 agrobusiness sectors of 21 sectors considered, mainly soya, animal feed, vegetal oils, coffee, meat and meat products.

(iv) gains in the trade balance in 8 industrial sectors of 21 sectors considered, mainly leather products, petroleum products; and

(v) losses in the trade balance of paper and pulp, chemical, non-metallic products, motor vehicles and components, machinery and electronic products.

Conclusion of a U.S.-EU TTIP without Brazilian integration into pan-Atlantic commerce will represent a serious threat to Brazil. Not only will Brazil lose international markets, it will be left behind in the negotiations of international trade rules. It will lose its present role as relevant global rule-maker and assume a secondary role as passive rule-taker.

In a time of global value chains, Brazil's integration with these two major economies is fundamental to the survival of Brazilian industry.

The analysis presented in this chapter shows clearly that the negotiation of an agreement between Brazil and the EU, now in its final phase, is an important step forward and should be concluded rapidly, before the finalization of the TTIP negotiations.

But a second step should also be considered seriously—that of an agreement with the United States. There is no "trade logic" in an agreement with the EU without an agreement with the United States in the case of a succesfull TTIP.

With the TTIP, a new opportunity is open to Brazil. It is time for Brazil to review its priorities and to reevaluate losses and gains. The costs of Brazil's isolation in the world because of Mercosul's difficulties should be re-examined with care. It is time for action!

Technical Annex

Simulations on the Impact of TTIP for Brazil

The GTAP computable general equilibrium model was used in the simulations to evaluate the first round effects of the costs and opportunities for Brazil of the conclusion of the TTIP.[12] The GTAP model is a global comparative static applied general equilibrium model. The model identifies 57 sectors in 153 regions of the world. Its system of equations is based on microeconomic foundations providing a detailed specification of household and perfect competitive firm behavior within individual regions and trade linkages between regions. In addition to trade flows the GTAP model also recognizes global transportation costs.

The GTAP model qualifies as a Johansen-type model. This model estimates the impacts of external shocks (gains and losses of a PTA) through a comparative static modeling (before and after the shock). The solutions are obtained by solving the system of linearized equations of the model. A typical result shows the percentage change in the set of endogenous variables (GDP, exports and imports, exchange rate and land value) after a policy shock is carried out, compared to their values in the initial equilibrium, in a given environment. The schematic presentation of Johansen solutions for such models is standard in the literature.[13]

The GTAP 8 database combines detailed bilateral trade, transport and protection data characterizing economic linkages among 129 regions, together with individual country input-output data bases which account for inter-sectorial linkages within regions. The dataset is harmonized and completed with additional sources to provide the

---

[12]For a description of the standard GTAP model, see Hertel, T.W., *Global Trade Analysis: Modeling and Applications.* Cambridge: Cambridge University Press, 1997.

[13]See Dixon, P. B., Parmenter, B. R., Powell, A. A., & Wilcoxen, P. J., "Notes and Problems in Applied General Equilibrium Economics," in C. J. Bliss & M. D. Intriligator (eds.), *Advanced Textbooks in Economics* (Vol. 32). Amsterdam: North-Holland, 1992; and Dixon, P. B.,& Parmenter, B. R., "Computable general equilibrium modelling for policy analysis and forecasting," in H. M. Amman, D. A. Kendrick, & J. Rust (eds.), *Handbook of computational economics* (Vol. 1, pp. 3–85). Amsterdam: Elsevier, 1996.

most accurate description of the world economy in 2007 (the last available data base for GTAP).

The main applied protection data used in the GTAP 8 data base originates from ITC's MacMap database, which contains exhaustive information at the tariff line level. The ITC database includes the United Nations Conference on Trade and Development's (UNC-TAD's) Trade Analysis and information system (TRAINS) data base, to which ITC staff added their own data. The model transforms all specific tariffs in ad valorem tariffs.

In order to capture the first round effects, the simulations were carried out using a standard GTAP hypothesis, which considers perfect factor mobility for labor and capital and imperfect factor mobility for land and natural resources. National aggregate supply of factors of production is exogenous and production technology for firms is given.

The way the economy variables are affected by horizontal reductions in bilateral import tariffs of the TTIP partners will depend on the resulting behavior of domestic relative prices. Domestic relative prices of the TTIP partners will be altered in such a way that import competition from the PTA partner will be favored, as the economy becomes more preferentially open to trade. Overall efficiency in resource allocation tends to be improved and, by the same token, possible gains from trade may take national welfare a step up.

Notwithstanding the aggregate benefits from improved resource allocation, regions might be adversely affected through re-orientation of trade flows—trade diversion—as relative accessibility changes in the system. Thus bilateral aggregate gains from trade are not necessarily accompanied by generalized regional gains in welfare. This issue of trade diversion versus trade creation has been an important one in the international trade literature, especially in the case of welfare evaluations of preferential trade agreements.

Chapter 6

Asia's Pivot to the Atlantic: Implications for the United States and Europe

Daniel S. Hamilton[1]

As Atlantic powers consider how to pivot to Asia, they would do well to understand how Asian powers are pivoting to the Atlantic. Transatlantic strategies to address Asia's rise should not focus solely on dynamics in the "Asian Hemisphere," they should also consider the implications of Asia's growing engagement in the "Atlantic Hemisphere"—North and South America, Europe, and Africa.[2]

This chapter looks at Asia's pivot to the Atlantic. It compares and contrasts the diverse motivations driving particular Asian countries to engage in the Atlantic Hemisphere. It explores the impact of these trends on Europe and North America, as well as on their own respective relations with Latin American and African countries; the extent to which North Atlantic partners have shared or differing interests with regard to Asian activities in the Atlantic Hemisphere, and how they should address growing Asian influence. The chapter addresses the economic, energy, security and diplomatic dimensions of these changing connections, and offers recommendations for U.S. and European decision makers and opinion leaders.

---

[1]This chapter is adapted from a related contribution by the author to Hans Binnendijk, ed., *A Transatlantic Pivot to Asia: Towards New Trilateral Partnerships*. Washington, DC: Center for Transatlantic Relations, 2014.

[2]Kishore Mahbubani's assertion that there is an "Asian Hemisphere" means by definition that there is also an Atlantic Hemisphere. This chapter explores the Asian Hemisphere's engagement in the Atlantic Hemisphere, and implications for the United States and Europe, as well as other Atlantic actors. See Kishore Mahbubani, *The New Asian Hemisphere: The Irresistible Shift of Global Power to the East* . New York: PublicAffairs, 2008. Unless otherwise stated, "Asia" refers to all of the region, which according to the aggregated data of the WTO classification includes the following countries: Afghanistan, Australia, Bangladesh, Bhutan, Brunei, Cambodia, China, Fiji, Hong Kong, India, Indonesia, Japan, (South) Korea, Laos, Macao, Malaysia, Maldives, Mongolia, Myanmar, Nepal, New Zealand, Pakistan, Papua New Guinea, Philippines, Samoa, Singapore, the Solomon Islands, Sri Lanka, Taiwan, Thailand, Tonga, Vanuatu, Viet Nam.

Atlantic-Pacific Dynamics

The rise of the Pacific is increasingly influencing pan-Atlantic dynamics in a number of ways. First, trade between Atlantic and non-Atlantic markets has boomed. China in particular has become an important trading partner for all Atlantic continents, and China's trade with Africa and Latin America has grown faster than with North America and Europe. Yet the trade of both southern Atlantic continents with most Asian countries, not only China but India, South Korea, Singapore and Malaysia, resembles traditional colonial patterns. For instance, about 90% of Brazilian exports to China consists of commodities, while 90% of Brazilian imports from China consists of manufactured goods. The pattern is similar throughout Africa and Latin America. South-North Atlantic trade, in contrast, is far more complementary; Brazil's merchandise trade with the United States is evenly balanced between commodities and manufactured goods. Such imbalances are provoking questions on both southern continents about the value of becoming locked into colonial-style trading relationships at a time when countries on each continent are working to diversify their respective economies, and when both Europe and the U.S. have lost ground in their respective economic ties in the South Atlantic.

Second, booming Atlantic-Pacific sea trade has created new port facilities throughout the Atlantic Basin, especially along its southern shores, and more are coming. The Panama Canal is marking its 100th birthday in 2014 by doubling its capacity, expanding ocean-to-ocean connections and altering global shipping patterns—and China controls the leases at both ends of the Canal. Large new deepwater port facilities are being developed in Santos, Suape, and Açu in Brazil; at Lobito in Angola; and at Walvis Bay in Namibia. Spain's Algeciras and Morocco's massive Tanger-Med complex are growing in importance, and port cities along the Gulf of Mexico and the U.S. east coast are scrambling to revamp their infrastructure to berth megaships coming from and going to the Pacific and other Atlantic destinations.[3]

Third, melting ice in the Arctic Ocean is opening new and shorter shipping routes from East Asia to and from Eastern North America

---

[3] *A New Atlantic Community: Generating Growth, Human Development and Security in the Atlantic Hemisphere*, by the Eminent Persons of the Atlantic Basin Initiative. Washington DC, Center for Transatlantic Relations, 2014.

and Europe. The U.S. government estimates that cargo transport via the Northern Sea Route alone will increase from 1.8 million tons in 2010 to 64 million tons by 2020. This is already changing commercial shipping patterns and has boosted both Atlantic and Pacific attention to Arctic issues. In 2012, 46 vessels carried more than 1.2 million tons of cargo through the Northern Sea Route, up 53% compared with 2011. In 2010, only four vessels used the route. Chinese analysts predict that by 2020 up to 15% of China's foreign trade between will be transported through the Northern Sea Route. South Korea's Vice Minister for Foreign Affairs has estimated that travel time and distance between the shipping hubs of Busan and Rotterdam will reduced by about 30%, referring to the new route as the "Silk Road of the Twenty-First Century."[4]

These changing Atlantic-Pacific trade patterns have captured the headlines and the attention of pundits and policymakers, yet they paint only a partial picture, since Asia's presence in the Atlantic Hemisphere is perhaps as significant in terms of its growing foreign direct investment, or FDI. While more Asian FDI flows within Asia than to any individual Atlantic continent, Asian FDI in the Atlantic Hemisphere is actually greater than in the Asian Hemisphere.[5] Asian companies are increasingly seeking resources in South and Central America and Africa, while profiting from open investment regimes in North Atlantic countries.

Asia's Changing Presence in the North Atlantic

First some perspective. Table 1 shows that Asia's overall FDI in North America at the end of 2012 of $484 billion was 62% of North

[4]Trude Petterson, "China Starts Commercial Use of Northern Sea Route," *Barents Observer*, March 14, 2014; Page Wilson, "Asia Eyes the Arctic," *The Diplomat*, August 26, 2013.

[5]See the chapter by Daniel S. Hamilton and Joseph P. Quinlan, "Commercial Ties in the Atlantic Basin: The Evolving Role of Services and Investment," in this volume. The World Bank defines foreign direct investment as the net inflows of investment to acquire a lasting management interest (10 percent or more of voting stock) in an enterprise operating in an economy other than that of the investor. It is "the sum of equity capital, reinvestment of earnings, other long-term capital, and short-term capital as shown in the balance of payments." According to the OECD, "lasting interest" implies "the existence of a long-term relationship between the direct investor and the enterprise and significant degree of influence by the direct investor on the management of the enterprise." See also http://epthinktank.eu/2013/04/25/chinese-investment-in-europe/.

Table 1. Foreign Direct Investment: Inward, 2012

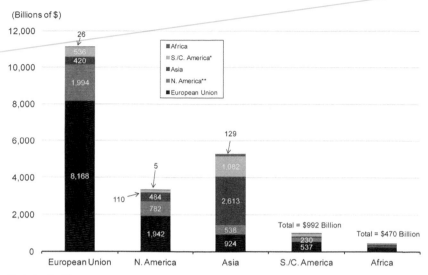

*includes Caribbean
**U.S., Canada, Mexico.
Source: International Monetary Fund: Coordinated Direct Investment Survey.

America's own cross-border FDI and a quarter of EU FDI in North America. Asian FDI in the EU is about one-fifth of North American FDI in the EU and about 78% of investment from South and Central America., including from offshore Caribbean havens.

Japanese companies are the major source of Asian FDI in North America and Europe. In the 1980s and 1990s Japanese firms boosted their investment presence in North Atlantic economies, partially in response to a stronger yen and to sidestep bilateral trade disputes, but also to tap technological know-how and innovation and to access more effectively the large and prosperous markets of the West. While this attracted considerable political attention at the time, such investments have since become almost routine; on the whole Japanese companies are relatively well-integrated into the European and North American economies.

Japanese investments to Europe and the United States subsided for a time, but have surged again in the wake of the financial crisis in the West and as other factors, such as an appreciating yen, a stagnant domestic market and a domestic energy crisis, prompted Japanese companies to again look for investment opportunities abroad.[6]

Many South Korean firms have followed suit, motivated by possibilities to acquire or improve technology and innovation and to position themselves strategically within NAFTA and the European Single Market.[7] The Korea-U.S. and Korean-EU free trade agreements have further stimulated commercial links between Korea and the two sides of the North Atlantic. North America now attracts about 22% ($54.4 billion), and Europe 17% ($41.4 billion), of overall South Korean global FDI of $242.4 billion.[8]

Coming to America

Asia's FDI position in the United States, on a historical-cost basis at year-end 2012, totaled $427.7 billion, or 16% of overall FDI in the United States of $2.65 trillion and about 23% of European FDI in the United States of $1.88 trillion.[9] Japan accounted for about 72% of all Asian FDI in the United States. Japanese FDI of about $308 billion was second only to that of the UK ($486.8 billion). Japanese companies continue to invest in the U.S. economy; Softbank Corporation's 2013 acquisition of Sprint Nextel Corporation was the largest Japanese acquisition of a U.S. company in more than 30 years. About 34% of Japan's FDI in the United States is in wholesale trade; Japanese companies account for 79% of Asian FDI in this sector. 30% of Japan's FDI in the U.S. is in manufacturing ($93.4 billion); Japanese companies account for about 76% of Asian FDI in U.S. in this area. Banking and finance accounted for 22% ($66.4 billion) of Japan's FDI in the United States; Japanese FDI accounted for 80% of Asian FDI in the U.S. banking and finance sectors.

---

[6]McKinsey Global Institute, "A Yen for Global Growth: The Japanese Experience in Cross-Border M&A," August 2012.

[7]Jung Min Kim and Dong Kee Rhe, "Trends and Determinants of South Korean Outward Foreign Direct Investment," *The Copenhagen Journal of Asian Studies* 27(1) 2009, pp. 126-154; also P. Gammeltoft, "Emerging Multinationals: outward FDI from the BRICS countries," *International Journal of Technology and Globalisation* 4(1), 2008, pp. 5-22.

[8]Korean Exim Bank, http://211.171.208.92/odisas_eng.html.

[9]Hamilton and Quinlan, *op. cit.*

Australian companies represent the next largest Asian investors ($42.7 billion) in the United States; their investments are comparable to Swedish investments in America. They are followed by firms from Singapore ($26.2 billion) and South Korea ($24.5 billion), each comparable to Irish investments in America. 60% ($15.8 billion) of Singapore's FDI in the United States is in manufacturing; 69% ($16.9 billion) of South Korea's FDI in the United States is in wholesale trade.[10]

Asia in Europe

Total Asian FDI in the EU is about one-fifth of North American FDI in the EU of $2 trillion, but it continues to diversify and expand.[11] Japanese foreign direct investment in Europe has grown dramatically over the past few decades, extending into many sectors of the European economy. The stock of Japanese FDI in the European Union totaled €144.2 billion in 2011, about 4% of overall non-EU FDI in the EU, comparable to Canadian FDI in the EU. The main EU country recipients of Japanese FDI are France, Germany, the Netherlands and the United Kingdom. Japanese investment can be significant for some smaller European countries. For example, Japan is second only to Germany as the most important source of foreign direct investment in the Czech Republic, accounting for 16.5% of total foreign direct investment in the country.[12]

Other major Asian sources of FDI in the EU at the end of 2011 included Singapore (€67.3 billion), Hong Kong/China (€63.9/€15.0

---

[10]Jeffrey H. Lowe, "Direct Investment Positions for 2009-2011: Detailed Historical-Cost Positions and Related Financial and Income Flows," *Survey of Current Business*, September 2012, p. 80; James K. Jackson, "Foreign Direct Investment in the United

States: An Economic Analysis," *Congressional Research Service Report*, December 11, 2013.

[11]At the end of 2011, the United States held 35% of total EU inward stocks from the rest of the world. Despite the rise of other markets, Europe continues to account for 56% of U.S. foreign direct investment worldwide. U.S. investment in Europe is nearly four times larger than U.S. investment in all of Asia and 13 times more than U.S. investment in the BRICs. See Hamilton and Quinlan, *op. cit.*; and Daniel S. Hamilton and Joseph P. Quinlan, *The Transatlantic Economy 2014*. Washington DC: Center for Transatlantic Relations, 2014.

[12]Hamilton and Quinlan, Ibid.; European Commission; JETRO; Ivan Deseatnicov, *Japanese Outward Foreign Direct Investments: A Study of Determinants and Incentives*, Tokyo: Waseda University, February 2013, p. 44; "Czech Republic is center for Japanese investment in Central Europe," http://www.worldeyereports.com/reports/2014/2014_czechrepublic/2014_czechrepublic01.aspx.

billion), Australia (€34.3 billion), and South Korea (€33.1 billion). In 2011, the highest annual growth among these partners was achieved by Hong Kong (54%) and Singapore (12%).[13] Media hype about Chinese investments need to be kept in perspective; even though China's stocks in the EU grew almost three-fold in 2011, the country was still not among the top ten investors in the EU.

India's presence in the EU is more visible in terms of people than in investment; the largest foreign-born population in the UK is from India. Indian investment in the EU has grown considerably over the past decade, but these amounts are from miniscule levels, and even such rapid growth has barely made a ripple in the EU's overall FDI picture. Nonetheless, while China's outward investment has gone mainly to developing nations and to the natural resource and energy sectors, about two-thirds of India's outward FDI investment has been directed at developed nations, and in such sectors as manufacturing and services.

China in the North Atlantic

As companies from such Asian countries as Japan, Singapore and South Korea have built out their investment presence on both sides of the North Atlantic, they have elicited episodic concerns in the United States and Europe, but on the whole are relatively well-integrated. Chinese foreign direct investment, in contrast, has more recently become the subject of much greater attention in both Europe and the United States; for some a source of hope, for others a source of anxiety.

Since 2000, China has encouraged its companies to develop operations overseas with preferential long-term government loans in order to "go global." Whereas the first phase of China's "going out" (*zou chuqu*) strategy was to seek opportunities in the field of energy and resources, particularly in Asia, Africa and Latin America, changes in Chinese economic priorities at home and Chinese corporate strategies abroad, together with a stronger Chinese currency, have ushered in a new, second phase of the "going out" strategy, which is more focused than before on developed markets as a means to help Chinese companies move up the value chain, look for opportunities in high and green

---

[13] Eurostat.

technologies, tap additional talent and resources, better serve customers in overseas markets, learn the ropes of regulation in advanced
economies, and buy into established brand names and business know-
how and supply chains. As prominent destinations of this second wave
of Chinese investments, North America and Europe can expect to
receive a substantial share of the $1-2 trillion in direct investment that
China is expected to place around the world over the coming decade.
Signs are that Beijing will liberalize the outward FDI policy environment for its companies at an accelerated pace.[14]

Despite considerable media and political hype, Chinese outward
foreign direct investment in the United States and in Europe is still
minute, accounting for less than 1% of total FDI stock on either side
of the North Atlantic. Nonetheless, it is growing quickly, and in fact
Europe has been the fastest growing destination for Chinese investment since 2008. In 2010, Chinese FDI into Europe and North America in 2010 amounted to nearly 14% of total Chinese FDI flows, compared with just over 2% two years earlier.[15]

Direct investment by Chinese firms in the United States has grown
quickly since 2009 and doubled in 2013 to $14 billion, half of which
was due to the $7.1 billion takeover of prominent Virginia-based pork
producer Smithfield Foods by China's biggest meat producer,
Shuanghui International. Prominent commercial real estate deals
worth $1.8 billion included the Sheraton Gateway in Los Angeles, the
GM building and Chase Manhattan Plaza in New York, and the David
Stott and former Free Press buildings in Detroit. China has also targeted natural resources; its largest overseas energy acquisition was the
$15.1 billion takeover of Canadian oil and gas producer Nexen by
state-owned CNOOC in 2012. Beyond the Nexen deal, Chinese companies have invested an additional $17 billion into other oil and gas
deals in the United States and Canada since 2010. Financial services,

---

[14]Daniel H. Rosen and Thilo Hanemann, "China's Reform Era and Outward Investment,"
Rhodium Group, December 2, 2013; Thilo Hanemann, "Chinese FDI in the United States
and Europe: Implications and Opportunities for Transatlantic Cooperation," German Marshall Fund of the United States, June 2011; Thilo Hanemann and Cassie Gao, "Chinese
FDI in the US: 2013 Recap and 2014 Outlook," Rhodium Group, January 7, 2014.

[15]"The Second Wave," *The Economist*, October 26, 2013; Ting Xu, Thieß Petersen and Tianlong
Wang, Cash in Hand: Chinese Foreign Direct Investment in the U.S. and Germany. Bertels-
mann Foundation, 2012.

entertainment and IT services are attracting greater Chinese interest. Chinese acquisition of IBM's personal computers unit; the $2.6 billion acquisition of AMC, the second largest U.S. movie theater chain, by Dalian Wanda; and the announced $4.2 billion takeover of International Lease Finance Corp (ILFC) are emblematic of the potential for Chinese investment in these and other industries.[16] Commercial real estate has recently become the single most important sector for Chinese investment in the United States, attracting more than $3 billion between mid-2013 and mid-2014.[17]

These investments are turning into jobs. According to the Rhodium Group, Chinese-owned companies provided more than 70,000 full-time jobs in the United States by the end of 2013, a more than 8-fold increase compared to 2007. Still, that figure represents only about 90% of jobs provided by Spanish companies (85,000) and only 44% of jobs provided by Irish companies (175,000) in the United States.[18]

Chinese investors are encountering a less-than-hospitable environment in the United States. The failed $18.5 billion bid for Unocal by the China National Offshore Oil Cooperation (CNOOC) in 2005 made Chinese investors cautious about U.S. investments, particularly in sensitive infrastructure. The Dubai Ports World controversy in 2006 did not involve China, but it did highlight ongoing U.S concerns about the impact of foreign investment on U.S. national security. An October 2012 U.S. House of Representatives intelligence committee report said U.S. firms should avoid doing business with Chinese

---

[16]Hanemann and Gao, *op. cit.*; David Wertime, "Hard Target," *Foreign Policy*, February 27, 2014; Sophie Meunier and Justin Knapp, "Coming to America: Top Ten Factors Driving Chinese Foreign Direct Investment," Huffington Post, July 31, 2012; Thilo Hanemann, "Chinese Investment: Europe vs. the United States," Rhodium Group, February 25, 2013.

[17]Thilo Hanemann and Cassie Gao, "Chinese FDI in the United States: Q3 2014 Update," Rhodium Group, October 21, 2014, http://rhg.com/notes/chinese-fdi-in-the-united-states-q3-2014-update.

[18]Chinese investors are also ramping up community outreach and philanthropic efforts; for example, Dalian Wanda Group, the new owner of the AMC movie theater chain, donated $20 million to the U.S. Academy of Motion Picture Arts & Sciences. See Hanemann and Gao, op.cit.; Hamilton and Quinlan, *Transatlantic Economy 2014*, *op. cit.*; Thilo Hanemann, "Chinese FDI in the United States: Q4 2011 Update," The Rhodium Group, 2012; Thilo Hanemann A. & Lysenko, "The Employment Impacts of Chinese Investment in the United States," The Rhodium Group, 2012. T. Moran & L. Oldenski, L., Foreign Direct Investment in the United States: Benefits, Suspicions, and Risks with Special Attention to FDI from China. Washington, DC: Peterson Institute for International Economics, 2013.

telecommunications companies Huawei and ZTE because they posed a national security threat, and the U.S. National Security Agency's clandestine "Shotgiant" operation hacked Huawei servers and monitored communications among executives.[19] Nonetheless, Lenovo's 2014 purchase of IBM's low-end server business for $2.1 billion was eventually cleared by the Committee on Foreign Investment in the United States (CFIUS).[20]

In addition, in 2014 Chinese e-commerce giant Alibaba Group made the single largest initial public offering in history on the New York Stock Exchange. The Atlantic nature of Alibaba's move is underscored by the fact that investors do not buy shares in Alibaba China, but rather in a Cayman Islands entity named Alibaba Group Holding Limited, established by Alibaba founders Jack Ma and Simon Xie to circumvent Chinese foreign investment restrictions.[21]

Although there is some concern among European governments and publics about the security implications of Chinese investments, the overall environment is more hospitable. As a result, Chinese investment trends in Europe are more dynamic than in the United States. Chinese telecommunications equipment firms, for example, have spent more than three times as much in Europe than in the United States

Although Chinese investment still represents less than 1% of the FDI stock in the EU, it is growing very fast. Annual flows to the EU grew from less than $1 billion annually before 2008 to an average of $3 billion in 2009 and 2010, before tripling again in 2011, reaching flows of $7.8 billion in 2012, and still growing in 2013. According to recent estimates, Europe could receive about a quarter of anticipated Chinese global FDI of $1-2 trillion by 2020.[22]

---

[19]David E. Sanger and Nicole Perlroth, "NSA Breached Chinese Servers Seen as Security Threat, *New York Times*, March 22, 2014. http://www.nytimes.com/2014/03/23/ world/asia/nsa-breached-chinese-servers-seen-as-spy-peril.html?partner=rss&emc=rss&smid=tw-nytimes&_r=1. Huawei, has had to deal with the issue upfront. In addition to having withdrawn its bid for 3Com, a network equipment manufacturer, in 2008 and having had its 2011 acquisition of 3Leaf, a cloud computing company, blocked, Huawei has had to respond to targeted

[20]Hanemann and Gao, 2014, *op. cit.*

[21]Steven Davidoff Solomon, "Alibaba Investors Will Buy a Risky Corporate Structure," *New York Times*, May 6, 2014.

[22]Hanemann, *op. cit.*, 2013; Hanemann & Rosen, *op. cit.*, 2012.

Over the past number of years, the eurozone crisis and attendant recession has offered Chinese firms an opportunity to purchase advanced manufacturing assets, talent and know-how; modernize technology, and acquire stakes in utilities and transportation infrastructure. Chinese companies have gained footholds in the automotive industry, as exemplified by Geely's acquisition of Volvo, Shanghai Automotive Industry Corporation's purchase of Rover; and China's stake in Saab. Great Wall Motors is setting up local production in Bulgaria and BYD automobiles in Hungary. Chinese companies have made investments and purchases in utilities (e.g. stakes in Portugal's EDP and UK's Thames Water); industrial machinery (e.g. Sany's acquisition of Putzmeister in Germany); information and communication technology (e.g. Huawei in Hungary, China Unicom in the UK); financial services (e.g. ICBC in the UK); and transportation infrastructure projects such as airports (e.g. Germany's Parchim and London's Heathrow), railways (e.g. in Slovenia and Hungary), and ports (e.g. Rijeka in Croatia, as well as Chinese shipping company Cosco's expansion of the port of Naples, Italy and its €3.4 billion long-term lease to run the two main container terminals at Piraeus port outside Athens—one of Europe's largest gateways for Chinese goods). Chinese firms also spent more than $7 billion on firms in the oil and gas industry, including local exploration and production joint ventures (Sinopec-Talisman), local refining assets (Petrochina-INEOS) and EU-headquartered firms with global upstream assets (Sinopec-Emerald Energy). Sensitive to potential hostility to outright takeovers, Chinese companies have also shifted tack and shown a growing willingness to take minority stakes, which now make up 58% of Chinese deals.[23,24] Since 2012 Europe has become the top destination for Chi-

---

[23]While sensational deals often grab the headlines, they do not always work out. For example, Europe was shocked when Chinese consortium Covec won a bid to build a stretch of a major highway in Poland in 2009, but little attention was paid when the company pulled out of the deal in 2011, citing soaring costs. See also Central and Eastern Europe Development Institute, *Partners or Rivals? Chinese Investment in Central and Eastern Europe*, 2012; J. Clegg, & H., Voss, *Chinese Overseas Direct Investment in the European Union*. London: Europe China Research and Advice Network, 2012; F. Godement, & J. Parello-Plesner, *The Scramble for Europe*. London: European Council on Foreign Relations. 2011; Thilo Hanemann, "Building a Global Portfolio: What China Owns Abroad," The Rhodium Group, 2012; Thilo Hanemann and D.H. Rosen, "China Invests in Europe: Patterns, Impacts and Policy Implications, The Rhodium Group, 2012.

[24]http://rhg.com/articles/the-eu-china-investment-relationship-from-a-one-way-to-a-two-way-street

nese non-resource deals; by certain estimates 95% of China's new industry and services investment deals have gone to Europe.[25]

While China did not appear as the white knight rescuing fragile European governments who found themselves on the precipice of the European financial crisis, it did offer help at the margins. China purchased $625 million in Spanish debt and has pledged to buy Greek bonds when the government starts selling again. China has provided billions of dollars in state financing for key public works projects in Greece and Italy that support Chinese state-owned companies and Chinese workers, including a $5 billion fund to help finance the purchase of Chinese ships by Greek shipping companies.[26]

These investments have also created jobs. Employment numbers generated by Chinese FDI are not available for Europe, but are likely higher than the 70,000 jobs directly supported by Chinese FDI in the United States. Huawei alone employs roughly 7,000 Europeans throughout the EU. Overall these numbers are not high, but in the context of Europe's continued economic turbulence and high unemployment, such investment can be significant at the margin for some countries and some sectors of the economy.

Chinese companies now have investments in all 28 EU member states. Between 2000 and 2011, the older member states known as the EU-15 attracted more than 85% of Chinese FDI. But new EU member states in central and eastern Europe have since become more attractive, in part due to their role in the extended supply chains supplying the EU Single Market, their location as the western gateway for the "Iron Silk Road" project being promoted by China, and to Chinese perceptions that the political climate in parts of this region is more conducive to Chinese investments than in western Europe.

---

[25]A Capital Dragon Index, 2012.

[26]Irish authorities are trying to parlay their position as a major center for U.S. FDI into a competitive advantage with regard to Chinese investments as well. Officials and business leaders have opened talks with Chinese promoters to develop a 240-hectare industrial park near Athlone, in central Ireland, to create a "Europe China Trading Hub" where Chinese manufacturers could operate inside the EU free of quotas and costly tariffs, and U.S. companies could have easy access to the Chinese market without costly and time-consuming visa applications and travel. Irish Prime Minister Brian Cowen has announced that Ireland could become the "gateway" for Chinese investment into Europe. For more on the Athlone project, see http://www.independent.ie/business/irish/337acre-chinatown-hub-comes-to-athlone-26848974.html

Moreover, more Chinese FDI in the newer EU member states has been in greenfield investment than in merger and acquisitions, the opposite of the pattern in the EU-15.[27] China has also established a special diplomatic venue for economic and political cooperation with 16 EU and non-EU countries in central and eastern Europe, replete with annual summits, and between 2011 and 2013 pledged $61 billion in investments and loans to the region.[28]

China has singled out EU members Romania and Hungary for special attention. Chinese Premier Li Keqiang pledged $10 billion in investments and loans to Romania at the end of 2013.[29] In December 2014, China, Serbia, and Hungary signed a memorandum of understanding on a 370 km rail route linking Belgrade and Budapest, with construction slated to begin mid-2015. China also announced its intention to create a new investment fund of $3 billion that would offer loans financed by China's state-owned banks for projects carried out by Chinese companies in central and eastern Europe as a door to the wider European Union.

China has also paid particular attention to Ukraine, having forged a "strategic partnership" that included Ukrainian engine production for Chinese fighter jets and Beijing granting Kyiv access to $3 billion in loans to irrigate its southern farmlands in return for annual exports of about 3 million tons of corn to China. Although Beijing has employed similar loans-for-oil deals with other countries, the arrangement with the Ukraine was a first for China. Keen on meeting surging food demand at home, and now having relaxed its previous policies stressing self-sufficiency in grain, China is closely eyeing the rich agricultural potential of Ukraine, one of the world's leading grain exporters, and is interested in directly leasing Ukrainian farmland or enticing local producers into loan-for-crop deals. Russia's 2014 annexation of

---

[27]Central and Eastern Europe Development Institute, *op. cit.*; Sophie Meunier, "Political Impact of Chinese Foreign Direct Investment in the European Union on Transatlantic Relations," Draft Paper for the European Parliament, May 2012.

[28]http://www.dw.de/wen-announces-10-billion-line-of-credit/a-15911596-1; http://gov.ro/en/news/the-bucharest-guidelines-for-cooperation-between-china-and-central-and-eastern-european-countries

[29]James Kynge, "Ukraine a Setback in China's Eastern Europe Strategy," *Financial Times*, February 27, 2014, http://blogs.ft.com/beyond-brics/2014/02/27/ukraine-a-setback-in-chinas-eastern-europe-strategy/?#axzz2wpPv1aJy.

Crimea, however, crippled a $3 billion agreement with Chinese entre-
preneur Wang Jing for the first phase of a deep water port construction project there, and the change of government in Kyiv called into
question another $8 billion in Chinese investments promised to now-
deposed Ukrainian President Viktor Yanukovych at the end of 2013.[30]

Asia as Creditor

China's investment mix in the United States and Europe differs in
one other aspect. In the United States, Chinese FDI has come under
considerable scrutiny, yet China has invested massively in U.S. bonds
and in fact is America's largest foreign creditor. In Europe the situa-
tion is reversed; China has generally eschewed European sovereign
debt purchases in favor of investments in tangible assets.

In terms of portfolio assets, Table 2 shows that as of 2012, the EU
held triple the value of North American portfolio assets than North
Americans held of each other's assets in 2001, and about double in
2012. Asia's share was roughly equal to North America's own share in
2001; by 2012 Asia's share had grown relative to North America's
share, but still less than the EU's share.

The U.S. is considerably dependent on Asian creditors, particularly
China and Japan. As America's debt burden soared in the wake of the
financial crisis and wars in Iraq and Afghanistan, China and Japan
became the second and third largest owners of U.S. Treasuries after
only the Federal Reserve. Together they account for over 42% of the
$5.8 trillion in U.S. Treasuries held by overseas investors (China $1.3
trillion; Japan $1.2 trillion in January 2014). Their holdings are drop-
ping toward the lowest level in a decade, however, as U.S. investors
have shown greater willingness to finance a greater share of America's
$12 in marketable debt securities. In the past two years, Japan has
added fewer Treasuries on a percentage basis than at any time since
2007, and China has slowed its accumulation to about 3.1% annually
since 2010. That compares with an average yearly increase of 34%
over the previous decade. The reduction in buying is one signal that
the People's Bank of China believes it is no longer in Chinese interest

---

[30]Kynge, Ibid.; http://www.bloomberg.com/news/2013-10-01/ukraine-close-to-3-billion-
china-loan-for-irrigation-project.html; http://www.ft.com/intl/cms/s/0/a9c0db18-4554-
11e3-b98b-00144feabdc0.html?siteedition=intl#axzz2wpQpOePY.

Table 2. Regional Composition of North American Portfolio Assets, 2012*

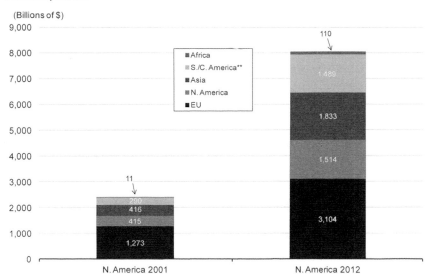

(Billions of $)

*U.S., Canada, Mexico.
**includes Caribbean
Source: International Monetary Fund: Coordinated Direct Investment Survey.

to accumulate such massive foreign exchange reserves, estimated at $3.8 trillion, more than triple those of any other nation and bigger than Germany's gross domestic product.[31]

Table 3 indicates that EU portfolio holders account for about two-thirds of portfolio assets within the EU. North America accounted for $3.487 trillion, about 2.3 times Asia's holdings of $1.514 trillion in the EU in 2012, but Asia's relative share is growing, as in 2001 North America had accounted for 3.4 times as much as Asian holdings.

China's portfolio mix in Europe is far more modest than in the United States. Estimates are that China holds €5.6 billion in the European rescue fund known as the European Financial Stability Fund (EFSF), and that across European countries overall China holds

---

[31]http://finance.yahoo.com/news/foreign-demand-u-treasuries-slides-152103025.html;_
ylt=A0LEVwkzGDBThAMAgYBXNyoA;_ylu=X3oDMTB0Yjkwb3VoBHNlYwNzYwRjb2x
vA2JmMQR2dGlkA1ZJUDM3MF8x; http://www.bloomberg.com/news/ 2014-03-23/for-
eign-grip-loosens-on-treasuries-as-u-s-buyers-bolster-demand.html.

Table 3. Regional Composition of EU Portfolio Assets, 2012*

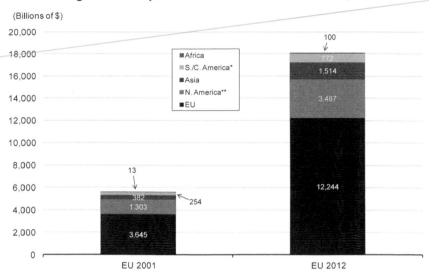

*U.S., Canada, Mexico.
**includes Caribbean
Source: International Monetary Fund: Coordinated Direct Investment Survey.

up to 7% of Europe's debt. China's reticence reflects its relative risk aversion in light of the eurozone crisis and Europe's recent economic volatility.[32]

Asia in Africa

Asian countries have substantially bolstered their presence in Africa in recent years. Asian actors share some common interests in the development of commercial, energy and resource opportunities, but the nature and depth of their respective interests differ, the depth of their engagement varies, and some compete with each other, as well as with Western and indigenous players economically, politically and even militarily across the continent and its adjoining waters. South and Central America. Most Asian countries do not have defined South

---

[32]Parello-Plesner, *op. cit.*, 2012; Hamilton and Quinlan, *The Transatlantic Economy 2014*, *op. cit.*

Table 4. S./C. America and Africa Foreign Direct Investment: Inward, 2012

(Billions of $)

*U.S., Canada, Mexico.
**includes Caribbean
Source: International Monetary Fund: Coordinated Direct Investment Survey.

Atlantic policies, but most have intensified and diversified their engagement.[33] Of course, foreign policy plays a role.

Asian investments in Africa, particularly from China, have been the subject of considerable attention in recent years. Despite these growing numbers, one must be careful to compare. As is clear from Table 1, the EU is the largest source of FDI in Africa, accounting for twice Asian FDI in Africa. Asian FDI, however, was 2.3 times North American FDI in Africa. In fact, South and Central American FDI in Africa is approaching the levels invested by North America in Africa—a sign of diminished U.S. attention to the African continent. Africa, however, remains reliant on foreign investment—the EU, Asia and North America all invested more in Africa than African companies invested in Africa.

---

[33]Adriana Erthal Abdenur and Danilo Marcondes de Souza Neto, "La creciente influencia de China en el Atlantico Sur," *Revista CIDOB d'Afers Internacionals*, No. 102-103, 2013, pp. 169-197.

Table 5. Regional Composition of S./C. America and Africa Portfolio Assets, 2012

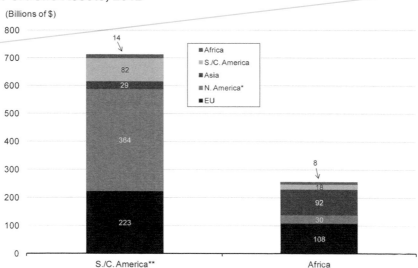

*U.S., Canada, Mexico.
**includes Caribbean
Source: International Monetary Fund: Coordinated Direct Investment Survey.

Asia's rise in Africa is more apparent if one looks at portfolio assets. As Table 5 indicates, Asia and the EU were roughly equal as portfolio asset holders in Africa, each accounting for roughly 3 times more assets than North America held in Africa. The trend is quite striking. Whereas in 2001 Asian portfolio assets in Africa were practically non-existent, they have risen dramatically. EU portfolio assets in Africa also rose 4 times in this period, but in 2001 the EU accounted for the vast majority of African portfolio assets; now its share is roughly equal to that of Asia. South and Central American portfolio assets in Africa have also grown to about half of North American assets held in Africa.[34] In sum, between 2001 and 2012 the EU's share of total port-folio assets in Africa fell from 71.8% to 40.7%, and North America's share fell from 15.8% to 11.4%.

---

[34]This includes money flowing from Caribbean havens, and so could originally be from Asian, U.S., European or other sources.

Japan in Africa

As other Asian countries step up their engagement in Africa, Japan has been scaling back. Formerly the world's top donor to developing countries, Japan now ranks fifth. In 2013 Tokyo pledged to Africa $32 billion in public and private funding, including $14 billion in official development assistance and $6.5 billion to support build infrastructure projects. Africa's share of Japan's official development assistance has increased, but the absolute amounts going to Africa have declined, and Japanese foreign aid is still tied to spending with Japanese companies or other Japanese organizations. Japan's trade with Africa in 2012 of $25 billion was only about 40% of India's trade with Africa, and its rather paltry FDI in Africa of $460 million in 2011 was only about 14% of China's $3.17 billion—and the gap is likely to widen further. Tokyo has declared its intent to is buy rare earths in Africa to end its dependence on China, the world's leading supplier of these minerals, yet has done relatively little to develop such industries.[35] Japan had been courting Africa in the last couple of decades as part of Japan's effort to become a permanent member of the United Nations Security Council. But as the impetus towards its bid has faded in recent years, so too has Japanese engagement.

South Korea in Africa

South Korea is also primarily interested in Africa's resources, although it does seek African support within UN and other international bodies. Africa is still a marginal economic partner for South Korea, accounting for only 2% of total Korean FDI and 1.85% percent of Korea's total trade in 2011. As with most other Asian economies, the foundation of Korea's commercial engagement with Africa is to access commodities, especially crude oil, in exchange for manufactured products. Seoul has also sought to promote the Korean model of state intervention as a guide to promote rapid and sustained economic development among African economies. It has focused on capacity-building in Africa's agricultural sector modeled on *Saemaul Undong*, an agricultural movement in South Korea initiated by the South Korean government in the 1970s, which eventually led to the eradication of rural poverty in

---

[35]JETRO; Javier Blas, "Abe Leads Fresh Push for Africa Riches," *Financial Times*, January 13, 2014; http://www.asianews.it/news-en/Japan-competing-with-China-for-Africa-trade-28073.html.

South Korea; joined with 15 African states to advance a three-year "Green Growth Initiative" emphasizing low-carbon growth, and has pledged to boost development aid to Africa to $1 billion.[36]

South Korea's reputation in Africa has been damaged, however, by accusations that its companies are engaging aggressively in illegal, unreported and unregulated fishing all around the African continent; and by charges of neo-colonial behavior related to a 2008 land-lease deal gone awry between Daewoo and Madagascar.[37]

Sub-Saharan Africa accounted for 26% of South Korea's Official Development Assistance in 2012, up from 12% in 2002. South Korea has traditionally used such assistance to promote its own state-owned companies in particular, but after joining the Development Assistance Committee of the OECD in 2010 Seoul pledged to untie 75% of bilateral aid by 2015.[38]

India in Africa

There is a long history of Indian communities in parts of Africa and the large Indian diaspora in countries like Kenya, Tanzania and Mauritius has facilitated closer economic relations. India has a common colonial experience with many African countries and has long ties with those that are members of the British Commonwealth. Indian energy and economic interests in Africa are substantial. India's annual trade with Africa jumped from $3 billion in 2000 to about $64 billion today, and is expected to exceed $90 billion by 2015. This is less than a third of Sino-African trade, but with similar growth rates, and India now ranks as Africa's fourth largest trade partner, after the EU, China and the United States. India's dependency on foreign oil, which stood at around 75% in 2010 and is projected to rise to 90% by 2025, compels the country both to diversify its sources from the volatile Middle East and to seek new energy sources, including in Africa. India now gets a fifth of its energy imports from Africa, particularly Nigeria. India's

---

[36]40 Korean investments in Africa have so far been limited to a few sectors dominated by mining sector, and with over half in Madagascar. See also Soyeun Kim, "Korea in Africa: A Missing Piece of the Puzzle?" http://www.lse.ac.uk/IDEAS/publications/reports/pdf/SR016/SR-016-Kim.pdf.

[37]Vincent Darracq and Daragh Neville, *South Korea's Engagement in Sub-Saharan Africa: Fortune, Fuel and Frontier Markets.* London. Chatham House, 2014.

[38]Ibid.

mainly imports commodities, particularly oil, from Africa, whereas over two-thirds of its exports consists of manufactured goods such as pharmaceuticals, machinery and transport equipment.[39]

This pattern has drawn criticism that India, like China, is engaged in "neo-colonial" relationship with some African countries, even as it has been a leader in the fight against colonialism. Yet in contrast to China's model of state-led, investment-driven growth and "non-interference" in internal affairs, India's model is based on support for democratic governments, private sector-driven investment, consumer-driven growth. Indian companies also tend to hire local laborers for their projects in Africa, while many Chinese companies import Chinese laborers.

Indian investment in Africa has increased markedly in recent years, especially in agriculture, energy, infrastructure, telecoms and mining, exceeding $35 billion in 2011. Throughout the first decade of the new century roughly two-thirds of India's African investments flowed to Mauritius, a critical offshore financial center for Indian firms. The stock of Indian FDI in Mauritius is estimated in excess of 20% of the country's GDP, helping it to emerge as one of the strongest in sub-Saharan Africa.[40]

India, like China, has instituted a duty-free tariff preference scheme for exports from poorer African countries, and has offered soft loans— but it does not attach conditions as China does. Africa is the largest regional recipient of India's Exim Bank's total line of credits. In part because India is unable to match Chinese aid levels, it has focused instead on capacity building in Africa. It is setting up scores of institutions in areas as diverse as food processing, agriculture, textiles, weather forecasting and rural development, and helping to build a pan-African e-network linking schools and hospitals across Africa with institutions in India.[41]

---

[39]Joseph P. Quinlan, "Growing Economic Linkages with Latin America and Africa: Key Drivers and Trends," in Emiliano Alessandri, et. al, *China and India: New Actors in the Southern Atlantic*. Washington, DC: German Marshall Fund of the United States, December 2012.

[40]Sudha Ramachandran, "India's African 'Safari,'" *The Diplomat*, December 2012; Quinlan, *op. cit.*

[41]Ramachandran, op., cit.; Daniel Large, "India's African Engagement," http://www.lse.ac.uk/IDEAS/publications/reports/pdf/SR016/SR-016-Large.pdf.

Like other Asian countries, India seeks African support in international forums, especially for its aspiration to become a permanent member of the UN Security Council. It has 26 embassies in Africa; China has 49. It has engaged in periodic India-Africa summits, as well as in different forms of regionalism, of which the BRICS framework is today perhaps the most prominent, although India, Brazil and South Africa created in 2004 the India-Brazil-South Africa (IBSA) Dialogue, which includes regular summits among the leaders of these significant democracies. As India engages more extensively with Africa and other continents, internal debates are raging about the country's foreign policy priorities, with some strongly focused on economic and security needs, others who favor the ideology of a Global South, and those who emphasize coordination with other democracies, across the South but also with North America and Europe.[42]

As the third largest contributor of UN peacekeepers in the world, India has a long history of UN peacekeeping in Africa. Current UN Indian deployments include the United Nations Operation in Côte d'Ivoire, the UN Mission in South Sudan and the UN Organization Stabilization Mission in the Democratic Republic of Congo. It has supported the African Union Mission in Somalia and the African-led International Support Mission to Mali. The Indian navy has also contributed to anti-piracy operations in the Gulf of Aden since 2008. With an eye to Chinese naval activities in the Indian Ocean, India has developed close security relationships with Africa's Indian Ocean islands and several African countries bordering the Indian Ocean, including Mauritius, the Seychelles, Madagascar, Tanzania, Mozambique and especially South Africa.

Malaysia in Africa

For all of the hype regarding China's activities in Africa, according to UNCTAD Malaysia had more cumulative FDI stock in Africa than did China at the end of 2011.[43] Malaysia was the third biggest investor in Africa behind France and the United States, pushing China and

---

[42]Dhruva Jaishankar, "India in the Southern Atlantic: An Overview," and Emiliano Alessandri and Dhruva Jaishankar, "Introduction: New Players in the Atlantic Basin," in Alessandri, et. al., *op. cit.*

[43]Global Investment Monitor, "The Rise of BRICS FDI and Africa," UNCTAD, March 25, 2013.

India into fourth and fifth positions. France and the United States also lead in terms of historical stock of investments in Africa, with Britain in third place and Malaysia in fourth, followed by South Africa, China and India. While official FDI figures significantly underestimate actual Chinese investment for a number of reasons,[44] Malaysian investment in Africa is considerable. Malaysia's portfolio of global FDI increased by more than five times over the past decade to reach $106 billion by the end of 2011. Of that, $19.3 billion was in Africa, which is equivalent to 24% of its total FDI. Trade between Africa and Malaysia has grown steadily at 22% per year in the past decade. The countries with the largest record of Malaysian investments are South Africa, Kenya and Nigeria. Malaysia has invested in agribusiness mostly in East and West Africa, but like India has focused its finance FDI on Mauritius.[45]

Dubai and Mauritius as Hubs for Asian Capital in Africa

Dubai and Mauritius have become key operational hubs for foreign businesses expanding their operations across Africa. In 2013, Dubai's trade with Africa was worth $30 billion, and outward FDI from Dubai to Africa in the past 10 years was worth $56 billion, much of it from Asian sources. $8 billion flowed into continental Africa from Mauritius, which continues to be among the most competitive, stable, and successful African economies. According to the World Bank, Mauritius is one of the world's most open economies to foreign ownership and one of the highest recipients of FDI per head of population. Its finan-

---

[44]According to David Shinn, "The official FDI figure for China in Africa significantly understates the actual amount for a variety of reasons. 1. It only represents FDI that is officially reported to the government of China. Some private Chinese investors do not report FDI flows. China's official numbers miss FDI that passes through Hong Kong, the Cayman Islands and the British Virgin Islands and goes to many countries, including some in Africa. 2. Chinese FDI statistics do not include investment in the financial sector. For example, China's $5.5 billion purchase of 20 % of Standard Bank of South Africa is presumably not reflected in the cumulative figures for FDI to Africa. 3. China has also made several large investments in companies located in countries outside Africa that have significant holdings in Africa. These investments would not appear in the cumulative figure for Africa." http://davidshinn.blogspot.com/2013/03/foreign-direct-investment-in-africa.html

[45]http://www.reuters.com/article/2013/03/25/malaysia-africa-idUSL5N0CH2QY20130325; http://www.trademarksa.org/news/huge-investment-potential-malaysian-companies-resource-rich-africa; http://www.themalaymailonline.com/malaysia/article/in-africa-malaysia-now-top-developing-country-investor

cial services sector accounts for 13% of the country's GDP. Money is also flowing the other way; Mauritius ranks among the top 10 largest sources of FDI into China.[46]

China in Africa

Foreign direct investment plays a key role in Beijing's "going out" strategy to secure strategic assets and natural resources to support China's transformation. China's hunger for global commodities has been stunning. It is now the second largest consumer of oil after the United States, and presently consumes 25% of the world's soybeans, 20% of the world's corn and 16% of the world's wheat. The mainland also accounts for nearly 25% of world rubber consumption. Name the commodity and there is a good chance China is among the largest consumers in the world.[47]

Nowhere is China's explosive growth more visible than in Africa, whether measured in terms of trade, investment, or Chinese workers building railways, roads and other African infrastructure. There are now around 1 million Chinese people in Africa, a figure which has grown from 100,000 early in the last decade.

In Africa, China is seeking to procure natural resources and agricultural products; expand and diversify its exports; and enlist the support of African countries for Chinese foreign policy priorities.

Africa accounts for about one-third of China's overall oil imports, and about 85% of Africa's exports to China comes from the oil-rich countries of Angola, Equatorial Guinea, Nigeria, the Democratic Republic of Congo and Sudan. Africa also provides China with 30% of its tobacco, 25% of its pearls and precious metals, 20% of its cocoa, 10% of its ores, and 5% of its iron and steel. China has also become the world's top consumer of fish, and Chinese fishing companies now regularly ply the waters of the South Atlantic. China is helping West African countries conduct "frontier exploration" in the Gulf of Guinea and has committed billions to upgrade Africa's rail network and information technology infrastructure to the benefit of ZTE and Huawei.

---

[46]Malcolm Moller and Anjana Ramburuth, "Mauritius positioned to cash in on China-Africa FDI," *FDI Intelligence*, August 14, 2013; *Financial Times*, August 2013.

[47]Quinlan, *op. cit.*; Hamilton and Quinlan, "Commercial Ties," *op. cit.*

Beijing has offered bundled aid packages, development loans and other preferential financing arrangements to facilitate the flow of resources back to China. Chinese imports from Africa, which tallied just $5.4 billion in 2000, exceeded $105 billion in 2012.[48]

Chinese companies are also seeking to take advantage of Africa's fast-growing markets. Despite many challenges, on several indicators Africa is better positioned than the Asian Tigers before their explosive growth in the 1980s and 1990s, according to Credit Suisse and the IMF. China's exports to Africa soared from just $4.2 billion in 2000 to nearly $75 billion in 2012. South Africa, Nigeria and Egypt ranked as the three largest African export markets for China; South Africa alone accounted for nearly one-fifth of total exports. China has borrowed a page from its own economic development by establishing and planning numerous special economic zones in several African nations. Just as the establishment of such zones in China helped fuel export-led growth and kick start the industrialization of the mainland beginning in the late 1970s, the same effect is expected in such African nations as Ethiopia, Mauritius, Nigeria, and Zambia. The Forum on China-Africa Cooperation (FOCAC), launched in October 2000, has provided an additional framework for cooperation extending to food security, health care, training and student scholarships.[49]

China now ranks as Africa's largest trading partner; total trade hit $198.5 billion in 2012. By comparison, U.S.-Africa trade volume was $108.9 billon. Research from Standard Chartered estimates that trade between China and Africa will hit $385 billion by 2015 The stock of outward Chinese FDI to Africa has also soared, from $491 million in 2003 to over $21.7 billion in 2012, more than a twenty-five fold increase. About 10% of China's new FDI has been flowing to Africa. The main recipients are South Africa, Nigeria, Zambia, Algeria, DRC, and Sudan.[50]

---

[48]World Bank. See also Christopher Alessi and Stephanie Hanson, "Expanding China-Africa Oil Ties," Council on Foreign Relations, February 8, 2012, http://www.cfr.org/china/expanding-china-africa-oil-ties/p9557, according to the World Bank; Alessandri, et. al, *op. cit.*; Shelley Zhao, "The China-Angola Partnership: A Case Study of China's Oil Relations in Africa, China Briefing Magazine, May 25, 2011.

[49]Deborah Brautigam, "Africa's Eastern Promise: What the West Can Learn From Chinese Investment in Africa," *Foreign Affairs*, January 5, 2010; Quinlan, *op. cit.*

[50]Keith Proctor, "China and Africa What the U.S. Doesn't Understand," CNN Money, July 2, 2013, http://management.fortune.cnn.com/2013/07/02/china-africa-us; Hamilton and Quinlan, "Commercial," *op. cit.*

Overall, Africans have embraced China's economic surge. Yet feelings of resentment are also growing, fed by shoddy construction, environmental damage and predatory practices, and there is concern that Africa could be locked into a commodities-for-manufacturing pattern in its economic ties to China. More countries are reviewing contracts with a critical eye, and some governments have raised their concerns in public. Nigeria's central bank governor has criticized the Chinese for exuding "a whiff of colonialism," and South African president Jacob Zuma, who has long cultivated Chinese contacts, has warned that the unbalanced nature of Africa's burgeoning trade ties with china is "unsustainable" in the long term.[51]

Africa's 54 countries constitute well over one-quarter of UN members. The continent has three non-permanent seats on the UN Security Council and is well represented in many international organizations, including the World Trade Organization. Beijing seeks to cultivate African countries, both bilaterally and in international forums, to support Chinese foreign policy priorities. Other Asian—and Western—countries, of course, do the same. In China's case, priority issues include Tibet, Taiwan and human rights. China has deployed about 3,000 peacekeepers under UN missions in Africa, joined international anti-piracy efforts off of East Africa, and displaced Russia as the largest supplier of arms to sub-Saharan Africa.[52]

China has been a staunch defender of the principle of non-interference in political affairs, yet it has also sought to advance its model of authoritarian capitalism as an alternative to Western models. There are internal debates in Beijing about the relative importance of each approach. As China engages more deeply in Africa, the policy of non-interference has become challenging, given the temptation to favor certain domestic actors promising advantageous resource deals, or dilemmas caused by the divisions and tragedies generated by conflict in some African states. And as some of Africa's "strongmen" have left the scene, Beijing now faces a new generation of African leaders, some of

---

[51]Dambisa Moyo, "Beijing, A Boom For Africa," *The New York Times*, June 28, 2012, p. A27; http://www.thisisafricaonline.com/Policy/China-Africa-engagement-Has-it-peaked?ct=true; http://www.economist.com/news/middle-east-and-africa/21574012-chinese-trade-africa-keeps-growing-fears-neocolonialism-are-overdone-more/print.

[52]Abdenur, *op. cit.*; Proctor, *op. cit.* Brautigam, *op. cit.* Taiwan now has diplomatic relations with only four African countries—Swaziland, Burkina Faso, Gambia and Säo Tomé and Principe.

whom are influenced more by notions of democratic accountability and the rule of law, and who may regard China's "non-interference" policy with caution.[53]

Asia's Evolving Presence in Latin America and the Caribbean

Asian investment, especially from China, has been far larger in Africa than in Latin America and the Caribbean (LAC). In 2012 Asian FDI in the region was less than half Asian FDI in Africa, although for countries like Japan and South Korea, LAC is a more important FDI destination than Africa. Like Africa, LAC countries have become more important to Asia as both as a source of raw materials and a new market for manufactured goods. And as with Africa, the underlying question is whether and how Asian and LAC countries might build out their relationships in ways that go beyond such basic commodities-for-manufacturing arrangements.

Moreover, as with Africa, headlines about rising Asian investments in this region must be put in perspective. In terms of portfolio investments, North America increased its portfolio holdings in South and Central America four-fold between 2001 and 2011, accounting for over half of the region's assets. As Table 5 makes clear, the EU was the only other major asset holder. The region's own holdings are modest, and both Asia and Africa are non-players.

The story with regard to foreign direct investment is shown in Table 4. The EU is the largest source of FDI in South and Central America. EU FDI in South and Central America of $537 billion in 2012 was 2.3 times the level of North American investment in the region ($230 billion), 3.4 times greater than South and Central American FDI flows within the region itself, and 8.5 times greater than Asian FDI flows to South and Central America. The eurozone accounts for 40% of all FDI in Latin America, the EU is the biggest foreign investor in Brazil, and São Paulo hosts the largest concentration of German corporate investment outside Germany.

---

[53]http://thediplomat.com/2012/10/non-interference-a-double-edged-sword-for-china-in-africa/2/.

Table 6. Asian FDI in Latin America and the Caribbean

*Data for China's outward investment in LAC for 2012 is a projection.
Source: Japan JETRO, Korea ExIm Bank, and China Ministry of Commerce; Totals do not include tax havens.

Despite all the hype about China, Table 6 shows that Japan is actually the leading Asian investor in the region, with $26.5 billion, and South Korean investments of $5.1 billion were almost 3 times more than Chinese investment in the region of $1.8 billion.[54]

Japan and LAC

Ties between Japan and the region have diversified from an initial focus on minerals and agriculture to encompass a broad panorama of trade, direct investment, and government-to-government cooperation that has shaped the development of sectors from automobiles and alternative energies to computer software and natural disaster preparedness, while helping to launch some key LAC export sectors. Trade between Japan and the region reached nearly $65 billion in 2012. During this most recent period, bilateral trade grew at an annual average of 13%, a growth rate that puts LAC-Japan trade below the

---

[54]*The Economist*, October 26, 2013.

region's total trade growth (14%) and well short of its dynamic trade with China (32%), but still ahead of mature markets such as the United States (9%) and European Union (12%). LAC exports to Japan were the most dynamic component of trade, growing at an average of 18% each year versus 11% growth for LAC imports from Japan. Japan's share of LAC's total trade is only 3%, having declined from around 7% in 1990. Likewise, LAC accounts for less than 5% of Japan's overall trade, a figure that has not changed considerably over the past two decades.[55]

Seen in isolation, Japan's trade patterns resemble the same commodities-for-manufacturing exchange that has characterized the region's overall trade boom with Asia. Yet trade numbers tell only a small part of the Japan-LAC story. As Table 6 indicates, Japan is by far the biggest Asian investor and in fact one of the most important overall sources of FDI for the region. What's more, its FDI is spread nearly equally across the primary, manufacturing, and services sectors. Even though initial Japanese investment in LAC was driven by the search for natural resources, Japan's FDI has diversified and grown, and in recent years Japan has accounted for 5-6% of LAC's annual FDI inflows between 2008 and 2012—and in some countries as much as 10%. LAC's share of Japan's total outward FDI stock averaged 6.9% a year from 2010 to 2012, up from 3% percent in 2005.[56] This stands in sharp contrast to FDI from China, which, in addition to being much smaller in absolute terms, appears to be heavily concentrated in the primary sector.

In many cases, Japanese firms have become major exporters from their LAC production bases, highlighting how the economic relationship is deeper and more diversified than indicated by simple bilateral trade flows. Japanese exports are less likely to be in direct competition with LAC exporters, given Japan's export profile, which is weighted more towards high-technology, capital intensive products. This stands in contrast to Chinese exports, which often pose a direct competitive threat for LAC exporters, especially in destinations such as the United States. Japanese technical assistance was critical in transforming

---

[55]Inter-American Development Bank, *Japan and Latin America and the Caribbean: Building a Sustainable Trans-Pacific Relationship*, November 2013.

[56]Ibid. In the 1960a Latin America absorbed a quarter of Japanese FDI.

Brazil's *cerrado* region into the country's agricultural heartland, whose production places Brazil among the world's leaders in exports of soybeans, maize and other grains. Japanese technical assistance and financing also helped develop Chile's competitive salmon industry.[57]

Strong consumption growth among LAC's burgeoning middle classes has attracted Japanese companies. Japan's free trade agreements with Mexico (2005), Chile (2007), and Peru (2012) have not only reduced tariffs and other trade barriers but have also encouraged direct investment and established mechanisms for governmental cooperation on a broad array of policy issues, although significant barriers on certain tariff lines remain. These countries are also all involved in the Trans-Pacific Partnership negotiations; a comprehensive TPP agreement would ideally harmonize the rules of origin and other regulations in these bilateral agreements as well as deepen liberalization in the sectors where barriers remain.

The Japan Bank for International Cooperation's LAC portfolio of nearly $500 million supports rural economic infrastructure, environmental protection and natural disaster mitigation. Its loan and equity financing to LAC has reached nearly $200 billion. The Japanese government has also worked with LAC countries to advance cooperation in areas such as environmental management, health, renewable energy, and infrastructure. Japan has a long history of engagement in the region and strong cultural ties through the presence of Japanese communities in Brazil, Peru, Paraguay, and elsewhere. Sao Paulo alone is home to the largest Japanese population outside of Japan.[58]

South Korea and LAC

South Korea has also been strengthening its presence in LAC, although from a low base. Bilateral trade of $2.5 billion is relatively small, accounting for just 2.5% of LAC trade, but it is booming, averaging 16% annual growth over the past two decades. Trade is geographically concentrated, with Brazil, Chile, Peru and Argentina

---

[57]Inter-American Development Bank, *op. cit.*; Kevin P. Gallagher and Roberto Porzecanski, *The Dragon in the Room: China and Future of Latin American Manufacturing*. Stanford: Stanford University Press, 2010; Mauricio Moreira, "Fear of China: Is There a Future for Manufacturing in Latin America?", *World Development* Vol. 35, No. 3, 2007.

[58]Inter-American Development Bank, *op. cit.*

accounting for most exports, but in terms of product mix bears closer resemblance to diversified patterns of exports to the EU and the United States than do LAC exports to China; manufacturing accounts for about double the share of the region's exports to South Korea than the region's exports to China. Korea's FDI share is relatively modest, accounting just over 1% of total LAC inflows and 8% of Korea's outward FDI flows in 2010—yet about 6 times more than Korean FDI into Africa.[59] Like their Japanese counterparts, South Korean companies have upgraded their investments in the region, focusing on manufacturing assets. And as with Africa, Seoul is offering its own model of development as a more relevant source of policy learning than that of China.

India and LAC

Indian-Latin American ties are in their infancy, but likely to accelerate as India seeks to tap into Latin America's abundant fresh water supplies and agricultural/energy resources. Between 2002 and 2010, Latin America accounted for roughly 4% percent of India's FDI outflows versus Africa's 12% percent share. Moreover, a large share of Indian investment in the region—around 70%—is invested in tax haven nations like the Cayman Islands and the British Virgin Islands. Indian exports of $13.4 billion to LAC in 2011 were 43% of India's exports to Africa, and Indian imports of $16.4 billion were also less than half of the $39 billion India imported from Africa in 2011. Brazil is the largest market in Latin America for Indian goods, while oil-rich Venezuela is the largest regional supplier to India, underscoring the importance of energy imports for India's economy.[60] Nevertheless, India's priorities will almost certainly remain closer to home than the seemingly distant Southern Atlantic.

China in LAC

Despite these broader and sometimes more extensive Asian activities in LAC, China's meteoric rise and its profound impact on South and Central America has eclipsed attention paid to the region's other Asian partners. China's soaring energy and agricultural needs account

---

[59]Korean Exim Bank, http://211.171.208.92/odisas_eng.html.

[60]Quinlan, *op. cit.*; Jaishankar, *op. cit.*

for China's rising investment profile in Brazil, Peru and Venezuela, the top destinations for Chinese foreign direct investment, and China is also engaged in substantial investment in the offshore centers of the Cayman Islands and the British Virgin Islands.[61]

The last decade has seen sharp spikes in Chinese investment in Brazil (where China's FDI stock rose from just $52 million in 2003 to $1.1 billion in 2011), Peru (from $126 million in 2003 to $802 million in 2011) and Venezuela (from just $19.4 million in 2003 to $802 million in 2011). Chinese FDI stock in Panama, particularly in transportation, totaled $331 million, larger than China's investment position in Mexico ($264 million). In 2013 two Chinese state oil companies, PetroChina and CNOOC, participated (with a 10% stake) in the winning consortium, led by Petrobras and including Dutch Shell and France's Total, for the right to develop, during a 35-year concession, the pre-salt oil in Brazil's Libra Field. PetroChina announced acquisition of $2.6 billion in Peruvian oil and gas fields from its partner Petrobras. In 2012 Chinese oil companies bought Occidental Petroleum's operations in Argentina for $2.45 billion. In sum, while LAC is not yet a priority region for Chinese investments, it is becoming an increasingly important part of China's energy diversification strategy.[62]

Since 2005, China has promised upwards of $87 billion in loan commitments to LAC countries. China's announced loan commitments of $37 billion in 2010 were more than those of the World Bank, Inter-American Development Bank, and U.S. Export-Import Bank combined.[63] These impressive numbers have grabbed the headlines, but closer examination reveals that most Chinese investment flowing to LAC has not materialized. The China-Brazil Business Council found that only one-third of announced Chinese investments in Brazil between 2007 and 2012 actually appeared; around $44 billion in publicized investments never were realized.[64]

---

[61]Quinlan, *op. cit.*; Hamilton and Quinlan, "Commercial," *op. cit.*

[62]Cornelius Fleishhaker, "Libra out of Balance—International oil companies indifferent to Brazilian pre-salt oil," No Se Mancha, October 22, 2013, http://semancha.com/2013/10/22/libra/; http://www.reuters.com/article/2013/11/13/us-petrochina-petrobras-acquisition-idUS-BRE9AC0CU20131113.

[63]http://www.chinaandlatinamerica.com/2013/07/china-latin-america-finance-database.html.

[64]China-Brazil Business Council, *Investments in Brazil from 2007-2012: A Review of Recent Trends*, June 2013; http://www.businessinsider.com/chinese-investors-have-soured-on-brazil-projects-

According to official statistics from China's Ministry of Commerce, Chinese FDI in Latin America has been only $5.7 billion since 2006—far less than the breathless totals bandied about in the media. This figure does not account for investment routed through Hong Kong, the Caribbean, or other tax havens. But it clearly shows that Chinese investment has been a major disappointment, especially in light of wildly inflated investment announcements.

In addition to the quantity of flows, the composition of Chinese investment has given LAC leaders additional reasons for concern. Chinese companies have been more than willing to make resource investments but not those that would increase capital stock or create value-added activities. 85% of China's investments in the region since 2005 have been in oil, mining, or agriculture. In short, China's overall engagement with the region remains a one-dimensional affair: the commodities-for-manufacturing pattern dominates trade, and Chinese investments reinforce that trend.[65]

Within this overall narrative, however, three subthemes are worth noting. The first has to do with Chinese ties to Venezuela. In exchange for guaranteed supplies of oil, China loaned Venezuela an estimated $46.5 billion between 2005 and 2012, 55% of all loans it issued to nations in South America. Chinese support was critical for a Venezuela unable to access international capital markets after defaulting on its debts. Yet leadership changes in both countries and deteriorating conditions in Venezuela have resulted in a dramatic decline in such Chinese largesse.[66]

The second area of note is an ambitious $40 billion project, ostensibly to be financed largely with funds from China, to build a new canal linking the Atlantic and Pacific across Nicaragua. The Nicaraguan

---

are-melting-away-2013-11; Theodore Kahn, "Chinese Investment in Latin America: Much Ado about Next to Nothing," No Se Mancha, http://semancha.com/2013/11/20/chinese-investment-in-latin-america-much-ado-about-next-to-nothing/.

[65]See the Heritage Foundation's *China Investment Tracker*. There are significant statistical problems regarding the total FDI coming into and leaving China, since a significant amount of such funds flow through Hong Kong, the Cayman Islands and the British Virgin Islands. Nonetheless, even with significant error there appears to be a substantial difference between announced investments and investment commitments and actual investment numbers.

[66]Inter-American Dialogue; httpwww.americasreport.com/2013/09/04/china's-pivot-to-latin-america; http://www.chinaandlatinamerica.com

Canal would have a larger draft, length, and depth than the Panama and Suez canals, and the Nicaraguan National Assembly granted a Hong Kong-based company permission to build and control the canal for nearly 100 years. It remains questionable whether this effort will go forward, due to ongoing differences between the Nicaraguan government and Chinese billionaire and HKND Group CEO Wang Ping—but it bears watching.[67]

The third subtheme of note is China's presence in the Caribbean, including sizeable flows to tax havens in the Cayman Islands and the British Virgin Islands, from whence funds can be and are being channeled to many other destinations. Much of China's post-WWII involvement in the Caribbean was tied to its diplomatic competition with Taiwan. Now Chinese state banks have established themselves as the leading lenders in the region, and Chinese FDI stock in the region totaled almost $500 million in 2011. Beijing has signed a series of bilateral investment treaties with Cuba, Jamaica, Belize, Barbados, Trinidad and Tobago, Guyana and the Bahamas, and Chinese companies have initiated ventures in more than dozen Caribbean countries. Cuba, Guyana, Suriname, and Jamaica stand out as the most important destinations for investment. In 2011, the Chinese national oil company CNPC began a $6 billion expansion of Cuba's Cienfuegos oil refinery. Chinese state-owned enterprises have also established stakes in Trinidad and Tobago's offshore oil industry. Activity by the Chinese government and its firms in global resource sectors reflects an effort to secure access to raw materials, including bauxite in Guyana, sugar in Jamaica, and palm oil production in Suriname; and lucrative infrastructure development projects, from harbor construction in Jamaica and shipbuilding in Guyana to rebuilding the main road to Kingston Jamaica airport. Chinese banks are financing the Punta Perla tourism complex in the Dominican Republic and the Baha Mar resort in the Bahamas, which alone has employed some 5,000 Chinese construction workers. The China Harbour Engineering Company is also nearing agreement to build a $1.5 billion transshipment port and logistics hub in Jamaica's Goat Islands, to take advantage of the expansion of the Panama Canal and growing Atlantic-Pacific maritime trade passing through the region.[68]

---

[67]Ibid.

[68]Kevin P. Gallagher, Amos Irwin, Katherine Koleski, "The New Banks in Town: Chinese Finance in Latin America," *Inter-American Dialogue*, March 2012; Robin Wrigglesworth,

Asia at the Poles

Asian countries have also exhibited heightened interest and engagement in the Arctic, in particular due to the implications of shorter trading routes between Atlantic and Pacific; the impact of Arctic warming on Asia-Pacific weather, circulation patterns and sea levels; and the potential for access to fishing and new resource finds. The U.S. Geological Survey has estimated that the Arctic contains 30% of the world's undiscovered reserves of natural gas, 20% of its undiscovered natural gas liquids, and 13% of its undiscovered oil—and that 84% of the Arctic's estimated resources are located offshore.[69]

The Arctic Council has now expanded to include as permanent observers China, Japan, South Korea, and India, all of which maintain their own Arctic research stations, as well as Singapore, and both members and observers are engaged in a far wider set of activities than was the case some years ago. South Korea has already invested in Canadian Arctic energy resources in the Mackenzie Delta.

As Arctic geopolitics evolve, one relevant development is the potential for Greenland's independence. Since its 2008 referendum Greenland is now largely self-governing except in some important areas, including defense and foreign policy. Momentum towards full independence continues, however, and seems limited only by the reality that Denmark still provides about half of Greenland's budget. An independent Greenland would recast the map of the North Atlantic as well as the Arctic. Denmark would no longer be an Arctic Ocean littoral state, the Arctic Council would gain a non-EU, non-NATO member state, the U.S. air base at Thule would be at question, and Greenland authorities would be focused on ensuring that their economy could support the burdens associated with independence. Some advocating independence look to the development of mineral and hydrocarbon extraction industries as a way to a more self-sustaining

---

"Chequebook Diplomacy," *Financial Times*, December 18, 2013; http://jamaica-gleaner.com/gleaner/20130913/business/business5.html; http://www.jamaicaobserver.com/columns/The-Chinese-Goat-Islands-offer-is-non-negotiable_16158194.

[69]U.S. Department of Energy, Energy Information Administration, "Arctic Oil and Natural Gas Potential," October 2009; U.S. Department of the Interior, U.S. Geological Survey, "Circum-Arctic Resource Appraisal: Estimates of Undiscovered Oil and Gas North of the Arctic Circle," May 2008; http://thediplomat.com/2013/11/understanding-chinas-arctic-policies/.

economy. In this regard, Chinese investment in Greenland is of some note. Chinese companies are already active in Greenland, particularly in copper exploration and mining.[70] Some analysts claim that Beijing is concerned that Greenland's increasing presence in the field of rare-earth minerals could compete with China's near-monopoly on some rare earths. South Korea has been particularly keen to develop Greenland's rare-earth riches; state-owned Korea Resources Corporation and Greenland agreed in September 2012 to pursue joint ventures with respect to rare earth elements, tungsten and cobalt.[71]

Iceland is another northern territory that has garnered Chinese attention. In 2010, China provided Iceland with a $500 million-plus currency swap to support the struggling Iceland bank system; in April 2013 Iceland became the first European country to sign a free trade agreement with China; and the country has been the subject of other Chinese entreaties.[72]

At the other end of the globe, Antarctica has also garnered renewed attention from Asia, especially China, which has established at least three scientific bases on the continent, stepped up its domestic base of expertise, and indicated interest in potential resources at the southern pole.

Conclusions and Recommendations

As Europeans and Americans consider how to address Asia's rise, they should not only consider how to work jointly or in complemen-

---

[70]There have been uncorroborated reports of a $2 billion project for iron-ore production by a joint British-Chinese undertaking. http://www.nunatsiaqonline.ca/stories/article/65674 prospects_fade_for_huge_greenland_iron_mine; http://au.ibtimes.com/articles/284118/20120119/denmark-gives-access-arctic-minerals-rare-earths.htm#.UzcPckZOXQ5.

[71]http://www.icenews.is/2013/07/27/china-concerned-about-greenland-rare-earth-activity/; http://thediplomat.com/2013/08/asia-eyes-the-arctic/.

[72]http://www.mfa.is/media/fta-kina/China_fact_sheet_enska_15042013_Final.pdf. After considerable debate Iceland rejected a controversial proposal from Chinese businessman and former CCP International Department division head Huang Nubo for the purchase of 300 square kilometers of land for an "ecotourism center," replete with golf course, in a desolate strip of territory in the northeast of the country. Iceland's minister of the interior, upon rejecting the deal, said "it never seemed a very convincing plan...One has to look at this from a geopolitical perspective and ask about motivations." See Andrew Higgins, "Teeing Off at edge of the Arctic—A Chinese plan baffles Iceland," *New York Times*, March 22, 2013. Also Christian Le Miere and Jeffrey Mazo, *Arctic Opening—Insecurity and Opportunity*. London: IISS, 2013.

tary fashion in the "Asian Hemisphere," they should incorporate into their deliberations an understanding of how Asian countries are pivoting to the "Atlantic Hemisphere." In this regard, five aspects are worth considering. In each area the transatlantic partners also need to be aware of issues where their own respective interests are common, where they are complementary, and where they differ.

First, this review has underscored the primarily economic drivers behind Asian engagement in the Atlantic Hemisphere, which in the South Atlantic is focused largely on acquisition of and access to fossil fuels, minerals, and agricultural commodities, and in the North Atlantic on access to significant consumer markets, technological know-how and innovation. Economic engagement has offered Asian countries a basis for greater political interaction in some contexts, but Asian political influence is on the whole less significant than Asian economic influence.[73]

This chapter has also demonstrated that there is no coherent strategy behind Asia's turn to the Atlantic; Asian countries act as much as competitors as partners when it comes to their engagement in the Atlantic Hemisphere. Individual Asian countries often export their intra-regional competition with other Asian countries to areas far from Pacific shores, seeking to eke out marginal advantage or curry favor from third parties in support of their respective political and economic priorities. The nature and aims of their respective engagement, as well as their approaches to human rights, democratic governance, civil society and the rule of law, vary considerably. Moreover, many Asian countries are learning as they engage. As Elizabeth Economy and Michael Levi have observed, "China is not pursuing its resource quest with reckless abandon; instead, it is adjusting its strategy and tactics as it learns from experience, moderating its global impact in the process."[74] This offers opportunities for engagement.

Third, if Asian countries have no coherent South Atlantic policy, neither do the United States or Europe. Yet the peoples of the North and South Atlantic are engaging and interacting with each other, as

---

[73]See Alessandri, et. al, *op. cit.*, p. 7.

[74]Elizabeth C. Economy and Michael Levi, *By All Means Necessary—How China's Resource Quest is Changing the World*. Oxford. Oxford University Press, 2014, p. 8.

well as with Asia, in a whole host of new ways. Globalization has generated more connections among the four continents of the Atlantic Basin, and with the world, than perhaps ever before. Yet there is no framework for Atlantic countries to address the issues they face together, even though there are many such efforts in the Asia-Pacific region. Asian engagement in both the North and South Atlantic spotlights issues that the United States and Europe have neglected; areas from which they have withdrawn; and future challenges deserving their attention.

Fourth, Asia's rise is also affecting the Atlantic Hemisphere in a more global context, particularly with regard to worldwide norms and standards that should guide countries as they address contemporary issues. That debate should influence how the United States and its European partners engage South Atlantic countries, as well as those in Asia.

Finally, this review has also shown that breathless talk about Asia's global rise must be put in perspective. Asian engagement in the Atlantic Hemisphere is uneven. Some connections are thick, others quite thin. On most indicators most Asian actors in the Atlantic lag significantly behind the United States and Europe in terms of their overall presence, with some exceptions. Africa has been a greater beneficiary of Asian activities than Latin America, yet throughout the South Atlantic there is rising concern about the nature and terms of Asian, and particularly Chinese, engagement. Few mechanisms are in place in the Atlantic Hemisphere, however, for established and emerging powers to hash out the terms of their interaction.[75]

With these themes in mind, the United States and European states, either individually or collectively, should consider the following measures:

- **To act together abroad, get your act together at home.** Without U.S. fiscal solvency, economic growth, and job creation, without a better-functioning domestic political process, Washington is unlikely to be the type of consistent, outward looking partner that Europeans need and want. Similarly, Europe's protracted economic and financial crisis threatens to drain U.S. confidence in Europe and its institutions and derail American support for major transatlantic policy initiatives, including a

---

[75]Alessandri, et al, *op. cit.*, pp. 1-5.

"transatlantic pivot to Asia." The single most important effort each partner could make to improve its ability to act together with its transatlantic partner abroad—in Asia, in the Atlantic, around the world—is to get its act together at home. This is particularly important as the United States and Europe engage with Asian countries that offer different models of economic and societal development, because the normative appeal and continued relevance of the U.S. and European models for others depends heavily on how well they work for their own people.

- **Don't just turn to the Pacific, harness the Atlantic.** The rise of developing Asia has captured the world's attention, and rightly so. Yet this review of Asian activities in the Atlantic Hemisphere underscores that globalization, by its very nature, is not about one region of the world, it is about how different regions of the world are connecting. And for all the talk of the Pacific, it is important to recognize that the Atlantic Basin is a central arena of globalization. The well-being of people across this vast region is increasingly influenced by interrelated flows of goods, services, and energy, people, money and weapons, technology, toxins and terror, drugs and disease. Yet there is no framework for Atlantic countries to address the issues they face together, even though there are many such efforts in the Asia-Pacific region.

The United States and Europe should address Asia's rise not only by engaging directly in Asia but by strengthening the foundations of their own engagement. The Asian Hemisphere is the hemisphere of contested norms and principles among and between open and closed societies. The Atlantic Hemisphere, in contrast, is—admittedly with fits and starts—coalescing around basic aspirations regarding domestic governance. Across the Atlantic space there is growing commitment to promote liberty, improve the efficiency of markets, and to respect human dignity.[76] And the Atlantic Hemisphere offers diverse models of practice that can be relevant to broader global debates about effective and responsive governance.

---

[76]All countries in North America, the European Union and Latin America—with the exception of Cuba—are now rated partly free or better by Freedom House. Africa, too, has experienced greater democracy. In 1990 Freedom House recorded just 3 African countries with multiparty political systems, universal suffrage, regular fraud-free elections and secret ballots. Today close to 60 percent of African countries are now rated partly free or better by Freedom House.

Of course, across the full Atlantic space achievement does not always match aspiration. Setbacks abound and challenges remain. Yet a shared and growing commitment to democracy, good governance and a culture of lawfulness also positions the Atlantic Hemisphere as the test bed for how established and emerging powers can formulate shared approaches to ensure the legitimacy and effectiveness of the international rules-based order. Whether emerging powers choose to challenge the current international order and its rules or promote themselves within it depends significantly on how established democracies engage with rising democracies. The stronger the bonds among core democratic market economies, the better their chances of being able to include rising partners as responsible stakeholders in the international system. The more united, integrated, interconnected and dynamic the Atlantic Hemisphere, the greater the likelihood that emerging powers will rise within this order and adhere to its rules. The looser or weaker those bonds, the greater the likelihood that rising powers will challenge this order. In this sense more effective 21st century global governance, including how Asian states relate to such debates about governance—is likely to depend on a more effective— and thus redefined—Atlantic Community.

In short, stronger ties among North and South Atlantic countries are not only important in their own right; they can offer a framework to address Asian engagement on issues of pan-Atlantic concern while strengthening the foundations of Atlantic engagement in the Asian Hemisphere. The reverse is also true: without active U.S. and European engagement as pan-Atlantic, not just transatlantic powers, exclusionary mechanisms could emerge; new privileged partnerships or resource arrangements could be built; and restrictive trade deals or discriminatory financial arrangements could threaten U.S. and European interests. An Atlantic Basin Initiative[77] of one hundred Eminent Persons across the four continents of the Atlantic has called for a new Atlantic Community that erases the invisible line that has separated the North and South Atlantic for so long and gives shape to these emerging trends, not as an exclusive bloc but as an open global region. North America and Europe should embrace it.

---

[77] *A New Atlantic Community, op. cit.*

- **Address Asia's Atlantic turn in the context of pluralism, not containment or confrontation.** This does not mean excluding or neglecting competition or hard geopolitical considerations, but it underscores the importance of placing such considerations within the broader framework of interdependence. Asian countries are already Atlantic actors and in many cases are important sources of jobs, growth and economic development. A number are important allies and partners for North Atlantic countries. Yet there is concern, particularly in the South Atlantic, about dependencies and various operating methods. The United States and Europe should not seek to isolate or prevent China and other Asian powers from operating in the Atlantic Hemisphere, they should work with them and Atlantic actors to tackle issues arising from their activities, for instance how to move beyond traditional commodities-for-manufacturing patterns to make trade more balanced and sustainable; how to manage volatility in commodity and resource markets; and how to ensure that growth does not come at the expense of regional development or local manufacturing industries.[78]

- **Take advantage of the Atlantic Energy Renaissance.** Asian countries are so actively engaged seeking energy and other natural resources in the Atlantic Hemisphere in part because the Atlantic basin is recasting the world's energy future. An Atlantic Energy Renaissance is setting the global pace for energy innovation and redrawing global maps for oil, gas, and renewables as new players and technologies emerge, new conventional and unconventional sources come online, energy services boom, and opportunities appear all along the energy supply chain and across the entire Atlantic space. Together these developments are shifting the center of gravity for global energy supply from the Middle East to the Atlantic Hemisphere. Over the next 20 years the Atlantic is likely to become the energy reservoir of the world and a net exporter of many forms of energy to the Indian Ocean and Pacific Ocean basins. Already 21% of China's oil imports come from the Atlantic basin. Furthermore, nearly an identical share (around 35%) of all world oil imports now comes from the

---

[78]See Alessandri, et. al, *op. cit.*, p. 66.

Atlantic basin (including the Mediterranean) as from the Middle East. Heightened Atlantic energy links, in turn, could reduce the dependence of many Atlantic Basin countries on Eurasian energy sources and take pressure off their intensifying competition with China and India over energy from some of the world's most unstable regions.[79]

- **Create a private-public Atlantic Energy Forum** to facilitate and develop Atlantic basin energy trade and investment. The inaugural Atlantic Energy Forum of energy CEOs, ministers and former heads of government was held in Mexico in November 2014—a new beginning for Atlantic energy cooperation.

- **Create an Atlantic Action Alliance for Renewables Deployment and the Reduction of Energy Poverty** that would develop a mechanism for putting actual and potential renewables entrepreneurs into contact with finance mechanisms, regulatory officials and policymakers, technical assistance programs and facilities, so as to stimulate more rapid development. The Alliance's goals would be to offer advice for policy, locate potential niches, identify investment projects and financial resources, provide a link between small-and-medium sized enterprises and existing and evolving global support networks, and to contribute, where possible, to remove barriers to sustainable development. Asian renewables companies could be included in this effort.

- **Start an African Energy Initiative** with key African actors to spark the energy transformation of Africa, which is still characterized by deep pockets of energy poverty.[80] Expanding energy accessibility can reduce poverty and infant mortality, improve education, advance environmental sustainability, and accelerate economic growth and prosperity. Such efforts would reposition

---

[79]See Amy Myers Jafee, "The Americas, Not the Middle East, Will Be the World Capital of Energy." *Foreign Policy*, Sept/Oct 2011; Paul Isbell, *Energy and the Atlantic. The Shifting Energy Landscape of the Atlantic Basin.* Washington, DC: German Marshall Fund of the United States, 2012.

[80]International Energy Agency (IEA)D. *Energy for All: Financing Access for the Poor.* Paris, 2011; http://www.forbes.com/sites/blakeclayton/2012/11/09/the-biggest-energy-problem-that-rarely-makes-headlines/; International Energy Agency, *World Energy Outlook 2010*, Paris, 2010. The IEA estimates the cost of putting in place universal access to modern energy by 2030 at 48 billion dollars per year—only 3 percent of what experts expect to be invested in energy projects globally over the next sixteen years.

the United States and Europe as important African actors, while including relevant Asian actors within a norms-based framework.

- **Engage African, Latin American and Asian leaders, through various mechanisms, to promote basic norms of openness, transparency and accountability.**

  - **Advance a common approach to open investment principles.** This should proceed along different tracks. The United States and the EU should incorporate into a final TTIP framework a common stance regarding principles of open investment, building on their previous statements in this area, and act together to advance those principles when engaging third parties. This is particularly important in the context of separate U.S. and EU negotiations now underway with China on bilateral investment treaties. They should also ensure that differences of approach to national security reviews of investment do not undermine or offer opportunities to exploit such differences.

  - **Gain greater support for the Extractive Industry Transparency Initiative,** a global coalition of governments, companies and civil society working together to promote openness and accountable management of revenues from natural resources. Countries abiding by the EITI Standard agree to full annual disclosure of taxes and other payments made by oil, gas and mining companies to governments. While over 40 countries participate and the Initiative is gaining ground, many countries have yet to join.

  - **Define agreed standard operating principles by state-owned enterprises.** The increased importance of such enterprises—in financial services, telecommunications, steel, chemicals and energy, and other natural resources—requires new rules so that private businesses can compete fairly with state capitalism. The rules need not push privatization or roll back state enterprises, but they should require transparency, commercial behavior, declarations of subsidies, nondiscrimination and open procurement.

- **Engage Asian actors in differentiated dialogues on Atlantic Hemisphere issues.**

  - **Engage China directly.** Take up China's call for a "new type of big power relationship" by using the U.S.-China Strategic and Economic Dialogue and EU-China summit frameworks to elevate consultations on African, Latin American and polar issues, not only to raise concerns but to explore ways to coordinate on such issues as aid, development, technology, technical assistance and alleviating energy poverty.[81]

- **Encourage India's engagement** on Atlantic Hemisphere issues, while being careful not to overload expectations or to tout India's development model bluntly as an alternative to that of China. Identify practical areas for mutual support, for instance electoral best practices and foreign assistance.[82]

- **Coordinate more effectively with Japan, Australia, South Korea and other Asian actors** on common or complementary approaches to technical assistance, economic development, aid, as well as norms and standards.

- **Incorporate into U.S.-European consultations issues arising from Asian activities in the Atlantic Hemisphere.** U.S. and EU officials each engage with Latin American and African counterparts on issues related to Asia's rise, yet do little to consult each other on such issues, particularly with regard to Asian activities in the South Atlantic.

- **Ensure that the Transatlantic Trade and Investment Partnership, or TTIP, is part of an open architecture of international trade, and open to accession or association by third countries.** TTIP promises a boost to North Atlantic economies. But unless properly designed as part of an "open architecture," the partnership could hurt the trade prospects of other countries. President Obama and EU leaders should declare publicly that TTIP is indeed part of the open architecture of international trade. As the negotiations proceed, in time officials should outline future modalities for accession, association, or complementary economic agreements with other countries. The United States and the European Union have common interest in demonstrating that TTIP is about trade creation, not trade diversion.

---

[81]Vera Songwe, Yun Sun and Julius Agbor, "Obama-Xi Summit: Four Reasons Africa Deserves Attention at the Talks," Brookings Institution, June 7, 2013, http://www.brookings.edu/blogs/up-front/posts/2013/06/07-obama-xi-summit-africa-songwe-sun-agbor; Alessandri, et. al, *op. cit.*, pp. 1-5.

[82]Jaishankar, *op. cit.*

- **Harmonize trade preference arrangements for low-income African countries.** North American countries and the EU should harmonize their current hodgepodge of trade preference mechanisms for low-income African countries. Latin America could conceivably join in offering the same market access, building on preferences already given by some countries in Latin America, and on interests they have expressed within the WTO to improve market access for poorer developing countries. Such efforts should harmonize country and product coverage as well as rules of origin of current preferential arrangements, taking the best and most effective provisions of each respective program, making them compatible and updating the rules to the current trading environment.[83]

- **Work with emerging donors towards a new architecture for aid.** The international landscape for development aid has changed. Once-poort countries in Asia and the South Atlantic have became economic powerhouses and started their own foreign aid programs. New donors like Brazil fully understand and respect the importance of developing country ownership of assistance programs. They have a clear competitive advantage in sharing their own development experiences with emphasis on the "how-to" aspects of implementing development projects. South Korea offers relevant lessons for South Atlantic countries, and its contributions could be enhanced through more effective coordination with other new donors, as well as the United States and the EU. India has now emerged as a new aid provider, and has worked on various projects with both Americans and Europeans. Enhanced coordinated offers the prospect for more effective and transparent efforts for the benefit of recipient countries. A new aid architecture should arise in which "new" donors primarily focus on transfer of knowledge, while "traditional" donors focus on continued transfer of financial resources to poor countries that need external concessional resources. Donors old and new should implement commitments made in the Busan Part-

---

[83]See Eveline Herfkens, "Harmonized Trade Preferences for Low Income African Countries: A Pan-Atlantic Initiative," in this volume. Also K.Y. Amaoko, Daniel Hamilton and Eveline Herfkens, "A Transatlantic Deal for Africa," *New York Times*, May 8, 2013, available at http://www.nytimes.com/2013/05/08/opinion/global/A-Trans-Atlantic-Deal-for-Africa.html?_r=0.

nership Document; participate actively in the Global Partnership for Effective Development Cooperation; and participate in the International Aid Transparency Initiative.[84]

- **Encourage Asian countries to enhance their contributions to the regional development banks of the Atlantic Hemisphere**—the African Development Bank, the Inter-American Development Bank, and the CAF Development Bank of Latin America—as part of a general effort to encourage these countries to be responsible actors in the development of the South Atlantic.

- **Be open to good practice coming from Asia**—The APEC-Asia-Pacific Infrastructure Partnership is a high level body bringing together public sector, private sector and international financial institutions within APEC where each can bring its own expertise to bear. Ministers identify priorities, processes and resources; the private sector examines sponsors, contractors, short and long term financiers; and the international financial institutions bring experience, best practice, anti-corruption and other skills. This process is inclusive and has the potential to filter out investments that are unlikely to have desired local benefits. It may offer a useful framework for African, Latin American or even Arctic collaboration, or to give life to pan-Atlantic mechanisms within the Atlantic Basin Initiative.

---

[84]*A New Atlantic Community, op. cit.*

About the Authors

Deborah Farias is a PhD Candidate in the Department of Political Science, University of British Columbia, Vancouver, British Columbia.

Lucas Ferraz is a professor at the São Paulo School of Economics at the Getulio Vargas Foundation—FGV. He is the coordinator for Economic Modeling at the Center of Global Trade at FGV. His research areas include: international trade theory, Computerized General Equilibrium Models, global value chains and costs estimates for infrastructure and non-tariff barriers.

Daniel S. Hamilton is the Austrian Marshall Plan Foundation Professor and Executive Director of the Center for Transatlantic Relations at the Paul H. Nitze School of Advanced International Studies, Johns Hopkins University. He also serves as Executive Director of the American Consortium on EU Studies. He is the Coordinator of the Atlantic Basin Initiative, a public-private partnership of Eminent Persons, experts and opinion leaders who support sustainable growth, human development and security among the four continents of the Atlantic Hemisphere. He has been a consultant for Microsoft and an advisor to the U.S. Business Roundtable, the Transatlantic Business Dialogue, the European-American Business Council, and various think tanks and foundations. He has served in a variety of senior positions in the U.S. State Department, including as Deputy Assistant Secretary of State. Recent books include *The Transatlantic Economy 2014*; *The Geopolitics of TTIP*; *Open Ukraine: Changing Course towards a European Future*; *Europe's Economic Crisis*; *Transatlantic 2020: A Tale of Four Futures*, and *Europe 2020: Competitive or Complacent?*

Jorge Heine is CIGI Professor of Global Governance at the Balsillie School of International Affairs, Wilfrid Laurier University, and Distinguished Fellow, Centre for International Governance Innovation, Waterloo, Ontario.

Eveline Herfkens is a Visiting Scholar at the Paul H. Nitze School of Advanced International Studies and a Senior Fellow at the Center for Transatlantic Relations. She was the Founder and Executive Coordinator for the United Nations Millennium Development Goals Campaign, appointed by UN Secretary General Kofi Annan in 2002, and has served as Minister for Development Cooperation of the Netherlands; Ambassador and Permanent Representative of the Netherlands, United Organizations and the WTO in Geneva; member of the Board of Executive Directors of the World Bank Group; and a Member of Parliament in the Netherlands.

Joseph P. Quinlan is Senior Fellow at the Center for Transatlantic Relations, with extensive experience in the U.S. corporate sector. He is a leading expert on the transatlantic economy and well-known global economist/strategist on Wall Street. He specializes in global capital flows, international trade and multinational strategies. He lectures at New York University, and his publications have appeared in such venues as *Foreign Affairs*, the *Financial Times* and the *Wall Street Journal*. His recent book is *The Last Economic Superpower: The Retreat of Globalization, the End of American Dominance, and What We Can Do About It* (New York: McGraw Hill, 2010). Together with Daniel S. Hamilton he is the author of *The Transatlantic Economy 2014* and other publications on transatlantic economics and globalization.

Lorena Ruano is a professor of International Relations and the Jean Monnet Chair in the Division of International Studies at the Centro de Investigación y Docencia Económicas (CIDE) in Mexico City.

Vera Thorstensen is a professor at the São Paulo School of Economics at the Getulio Vargas Foundation—FGV. She is also the Head of the Center on Global Trade and Investment at FGV and Head of the WTO Chair in Brazil. She was the economic advisor of the Mission of Brazil to the WTO from 1995 until 2010 and Chair of the Committee on Rules of Origin for seven years. Her research areas include: trade regulation, preferential trade, trade and exchange rate, new barriers to trade (TBT-SPS), value chains and WTO.